# The Millheim

# and

# Cat Spring Pioneers

## German Immigrants Building a New Life in Texas

James V. Woodrick &
Stephen A. Engelking

The Millheim and Cat Spring Pioneers

German Immigrants Building a New Life in Texas

by

© 2017 James V. Woodrick & Stephen A. Engelking

ISBN: 978-1-9998691-2-0

Cover illustration:

This painting was made by Amalie Schiffer née Engelking after she had visited her brother Ferdinand Engelking in Texas in 1851. Her rendition of the Engelking cabin at Millheim was sketched during her visit and painted after she returned to her home in Germany.

# Der Stern von Texas

## by August Heinrich Hoffmann von Fallersleben[1]

**Der Stern von Texas**

1. Hin nach Texas! hin nach Texas!
   Wo der Stern im blauen Felde
   Eine neue Welt verkündet,
   Jedes Herz für Recht und Freiheit
   Und für Wahrheit froh entzündet -

   *Dahin sehnt mein Herz sich ganz.*

2. Hin nach Texas! hin nach Texas!
   Wo der Fluch der Überlief'rung
   Und der alte Köhlerglaube
   Vor der reinen Menschenliebe
   Endlich wird zu Asch' und Staube -

   *Dahin sehnt mein Herz sich ganz.*

3. Hin nach Texas! hin nach Texas!
   Wo die Pflugschar wird das Zeichen
   Der Versöhnung und Erhebung,
   Daß die Menschheit wieder feiert
   Ihren Maitag der Belebung -

   *Dahin sehn mein Herz sich ganz.*

4. Hin nach Texas! hin nach Texas!
   Gold'ner Stern, du bist der Bote
   Unsers neuen schön'ren Lebens:
   Denn was freie Herzen hoffen,
   Hofften sie noch nie vergebens.

   *Sei gegrüßt, du gold'ner Stern!*

**The Star of Texas**

1. Off to Texas! Off to Texas!
   Where the star in those blue pastures
   A new world doth proclaimeth,
   Ev'ry heart for right and freedom
   And joyfully for truth inflame -

   *For which my whole heart yearneth.*

2. Off to Texas! Off to Texas!
   Where the curse of old tradition
   And blind unquestioning belief
   Which when faced with selfless love,
   Finally to dust and ashes turns -

   *For which my whole heart yearneth.*

3. Off to Texas! Off to Texas!
   Where plowshare doth become the sign
   Of accord and ennoblement,
   As mankind celebrates once more
   On its May Day of revival -

   *For which my whole heart yearneth.*

4. Off to Texas! Off to Texas!
   Golden star, thou art the envoy
   Of our new more beautiful life:
   Then what free hearts doth hopeth for,
   Haveth never hoped in vain.

   *We greet thee, thou golden star!*

---

[1] Composed in 1845 to commemorate Adolph Fuchs departure for Texas. Included in 1846 in his published songbook Hoffmann von Fallersleben A. *Texanische Lieder*. Buchholz in der Nordheide: Uwe Laugwitz; 2001.
English translation here by Stephen A. Engelking. The melody can be heard at http://ingeb.org/Lieder/nachsevi.mid

# Preface

This book is a continuation of an effort began in 2015 by a handful of individuals with an interest in the history of the German settlements at Cat Spring and Millheim in Austin County, Texas. We began resurrecting obscure books, newspaper and periodical articles, literary novels and plays written about the area by former residents a century or so ago. Our purpose was to make an inventory of all such documents, ascertain their current status as to public availability and republish what we could of those still in the "obscure" category.

We loosely termed ourselves the Millheim Literary Circle. The core group of individuals at that time were Jamie Elick of Bellville, Stephen (Steve) Engelking of Tuningen, Germany, James Woodrick of Austin, and William Heaton of Calabasas, California. Each had his own special connection to the area. Jamie and Jim grew up in Bellville and are avid students of the local history. Steve's grandfather was born and raised in Millheim and may of his direct ancestors were co-founders of Millheim and Cat Spring. Will owns land in Millheim that he inherited from one of the early settlers, his ancestor Johann Severin.

In this book we present a brief history of the extended Cat Spring—Millheim community in western Austin County, along with reproductions of several articles written by early pioneers. We also summarize the significant literary works created by early settlers in the area, and reproduce herein some of these long out-of-print works.

    James V. Woodrick,
    Stephen A. Engelking

# Table of Contents

Cat Spring..................................................................15
Letters That Sparked German and Czech Emmigration...39
Millheim......................................................................73
Pioneer Settlers in the Cat Spring / Millheim Corridor....79
The Adolph Fuchs Family in Cat Spring............................99
The Cat Spring Agricultural Society....................................107
The Millheim Harmonie Verein............................................113
The Millheim Land Swindles...............................................115
Pioneer Times at the A. and M............................................119
Christmas in Troubled Times..............................................127
The German Settlers of Millheim Before The Civil War..141
The Schoolmasters of New Rostock....................................151
Life of German Pioneers in Early Texas.............................181
Robert Justus Kleberg, Yorktown........................................189
The First German Woman in Texas....................................203
Excerpts from Experiences and Observations....................209
Excerpts from A Boy's Civil War Story...............................219
Articles and Book Excerpts About Cat Spring and Millheim.......................................................................239
Literary Works by Cat Spring and Millheim Residents. .241
Bibliography / Related Reading.........................................243

# List of Illustrations

Map of Cat Spring Area inc. Early Roads...................................11

Map of Millheim Community c. 1860.........................................13

Sign in Cat Spring Hall................................................................30

Friedrich Ferdinand Engelking with Wife Caroline..................82

Carl Adolf Friedrich Fuchs.......................................................84

Robert Justus Kleberg..............................................................87

Ernst Gustav Maetze.................................................................88

Herman Nagel............................................................................90

Johannes Christlieb Nathanael Romberg................................91

William Andreas Trenckmann...................................................93

Johann Heinrich Vornkahl........................................................96

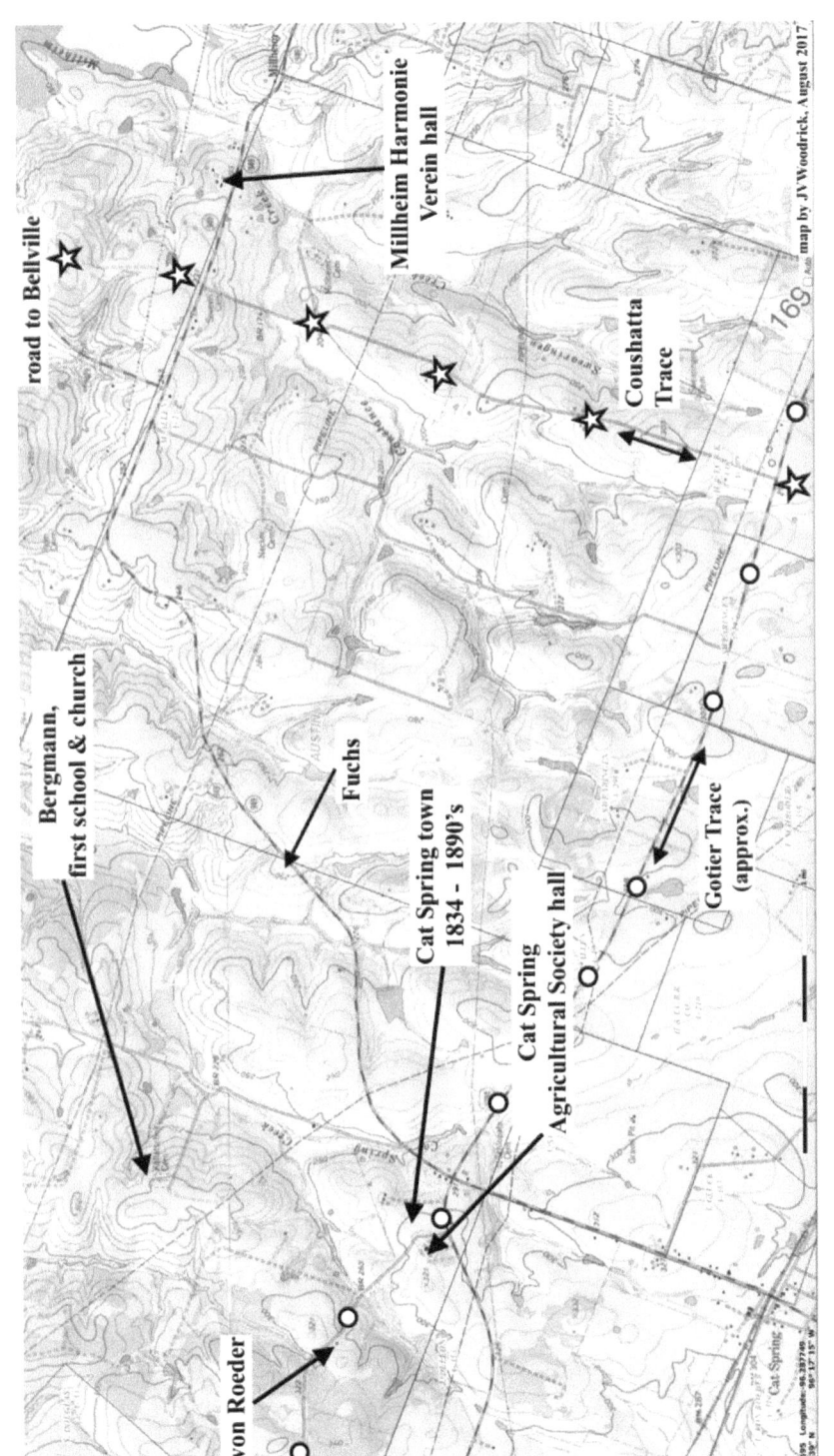

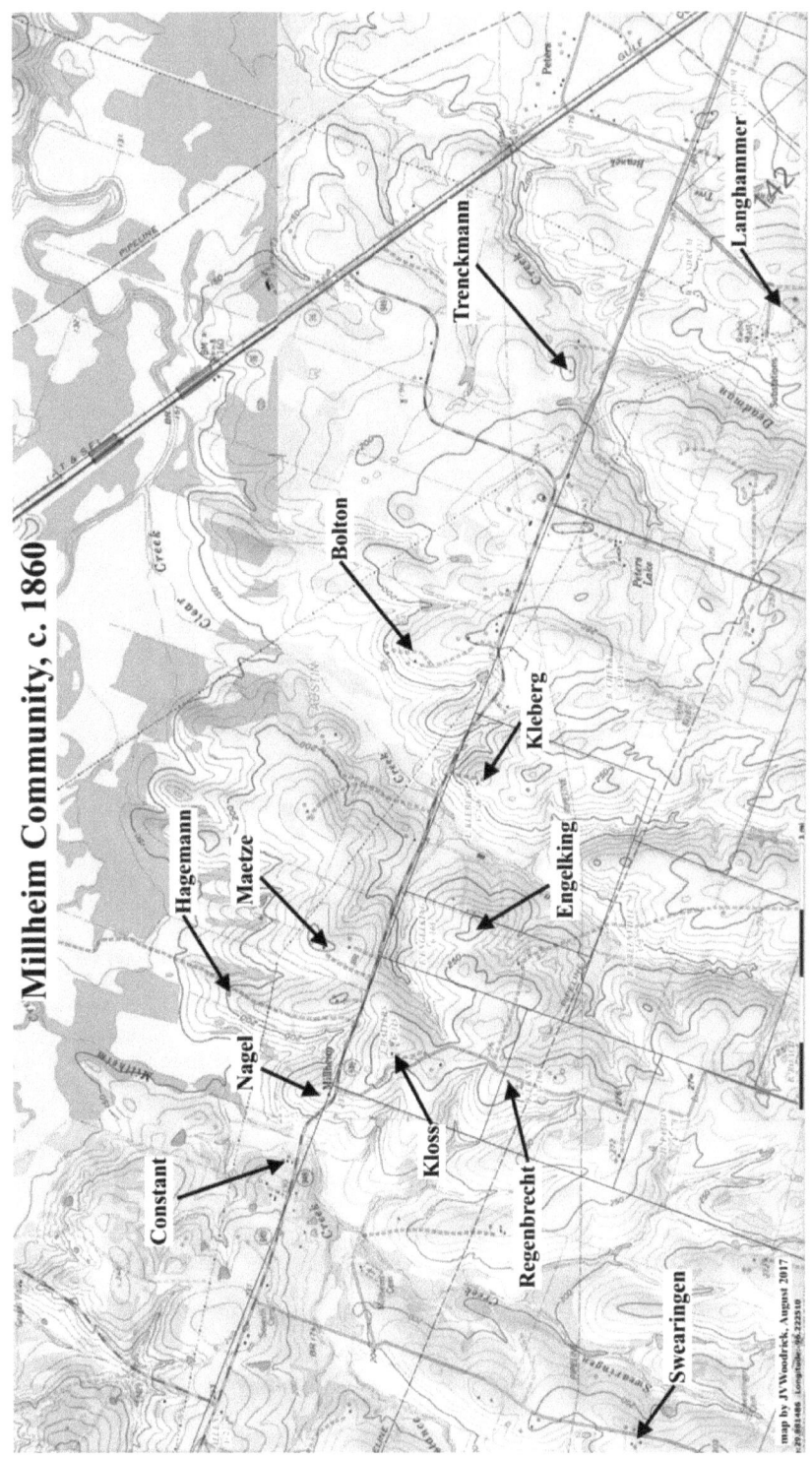

# Cat Spring

The first settlers in the area were Americans who came to Mexican Texas to participate in Stephen Austin's colony. Miles Allen received the first land grant between the Cumings "Hacienda" Mill Tract and the San Bernard River in May, 1827. Sion Bostick arrived in 1829 and was granted tracts on West Mill Creek and the San Bernard. Elemelech Swearingen arrived in Texas from Missouri in 1832 and was granted land on West Mill Creek. His two brothers Valentine and Samuel joined him in 1835 and were awarded grants near the Miles Allen tract.

Stephen Austin actively sought German and Swiss settlers to join his colony in Texas. He admired their character and work ethic, saying in a letter written in 1830 "they have not in general that horrible mania for speculation which is so prominent a trait in the English and North American character, and above all they will oppose slavery." He reached out to German officials about this proposal, who replied that it would be difficult to convince settlers to select Texas over United States territories then being settled, but if he (Austin) could attract a few families who came to Texas and liked it, he would have no problem attracting more. Friedrich Ernst brought the first German family to Texas; he had originally planned to settle in Missouri but changed his mind when he heard favorable reports on Texas; perhaps from Austin's outreach. It was Ernst's letter back home soon after he arrived that began what later became a flood of Germans moving to Texas.[2]

2  Barker, Eugene, Life of Stephen F. Austin: 254; Biesele, History of the German Settlements in Texas: 25, 26.

Cat Spring was founded in 1834 by a group of German immigrants who followed Friedrich Ernst, founder of Industry in 1831, the first German settlement in Texas. Ernst came to the area with Charles Fortran, who settled nearby. Ernst had settled on his land grant some 30 miles west of San Felipe, the seat of Steven Austin's colony in Mexican Texas. Ernst located on the newly-blazed road from San Felipe to Bastrop called the Gotier Trace[3]. His American neighbors soon named the nascent town Industry, describing their view of the "industrious" German settlers there. Soon after he arrived, Ernst wrote a long letter back home extolling the virtues of his new home in Texas. This letter circulated widely, and was responsible for many other Germans to decide to move to Texas.

The largest of contingent of the Cat Spring pioneers was the extended family of Ludwig Sigismund Anton von Roeder. They had read Ernst's letter and decided to make the move. Initially four unmarried children of Ludwig von Roeder (Albrecht, Ludwig / Louis, Joachim and Valeska) and a servant named Franz Pollhart were sent in early 1834 to scout the territory and begin planning for the rest of the family to join them. Traveling with them was a couple from Canton Aargau, Switzerland, Charles and Mary Amsler. All initially proceeded to the Industry settlement of Ernst and Fortran, but soon selected their land grants on the Gotier Trace about half way between San Felipe and Industry. Here, soon after they arrived, Louis von Roeder killed a "wild cat" (probably a bobcat) at a nearby spring and thus the settlement was named "katzenquelle", or Cat Spring. Into the 1850s it was referred to as "Wild Cat Spring".

The remainder of the von Roeder family departed on September 30, 1834, landed at New Orleans, and on December 22nd wrecked on Galveston Island as they approached the Texas coast. In this group were patriarch Ludwig von Roeder and his wife Louise, his daughters Caroline, Louisa and Rosalie with her new husband Robert Justus Kleberg, sons Rudolph, Otto

---

3  See *The Gotier Trace* by James Woodrick on his *Snippets of Texas History* blog, texashistorysnippets.blogspot.com

and William von Roeder, Otto's wife Pauline and her single sister Antoinette Donop, and Louis Kleberg, Robert's brother.

Robert Kleberg and Rudolph von Roeder went ahead to the mainland to locate the survivors of their advance party; they soon found Albrecht and Louis von Roeder, seriously ill and living on their newly granted land at what would become Cat Spring. The others in the advance group had died of yellow fever soon after arrival. The women were housed in Harrisburg for a few months while the men returned to the von Roeder land grants and, by September of 1835, had completed two cabins. By the end of 1835, all had moved from Harrisburg and settled into their new homes.

In October, news arrived of the Battle of Gonzales and the beginning of the Texas Revolution. Albrecht and Louis von Roeder and Charles Amsler immediately left for San Antonio where they participated in the Siege of Bexar and the forced retreat of the Mexican army there back to the Rio Grande. They returned home, but by the next March learned that a large Mexican Army under Santa Anna had returned to Texas, taken San Antonio and the Alamo, and was marching east to punish the Texian revolutionaries. Many of the settlers in Cat Spring and Industry were forced to flee in what became known as the Runaway Scrape. The Cat Spring group decided that Robert Kleberg and Louis von Roeder should join Sam Houston's army (they fought at San Jacinto) and the rest would flee with whatever belongings they could carry. When they returned home after the victory at San Jacinto they found their homes burned, crops and animals destroyed by the wing of the Mexican army under General Antonio Gaona who had marched from Bastrop along the Gotier Trace through Industry and Cat Spring en route to join Santa Anna at San Felipe. They soon rebuilt, and were joined by other new German immigrants who arrived and settled nearby.

Native Americans did not pose a significant problem for the first Germans to settle at Cat Spring. None lived in the area, and the nearby presence of many armed residents made raids too risky. There were occasional visits by various tribes, but these were nearly all friendly encounters in which goods were exchanged. The most memorable visit at Cat Spring was of Comanches in June of 1838. Robert Kleberg was living in Cat Spring at the time, and related this visit in his later years. One biographer of Kleberg stated: "He frequently spoke of one occurrence during his residence at Cat Spring, where a numerous tribe of Comanches passed by his house to the city of Houston to interview the President of the Republic of Texas on the question of making peace. He speaks of the appearance of these savages upon their return from Houston as most ludicrous. Many of them had adorned themselves with stove pipe hats, red ribbons and all kinds of fancy dress articles, all of which was in strange contrast with their usual wearing apparel. They stopped at the Judge's house on their way from Houston, and requested his wife to mend their flag, which she readily consented to do." The Treaty Between Texas and the Comanche Indians was signed in Houston on May 29th, 1838[4]. The treaty did not specify a line of demarkation between the Indians and white settlers, which the Comanches had wanted; it did require them to make annual return visits to Houston on the first of October. The treaty was never ratified by the Texas Senate.

Over the years Cat Spring developed into a town, with several residences and businesses located near the von Roeder homestead, just east of the current Cat Spring Agricultural Society hall. The Missouri-Kansas-Texas Railroad Company (the MKT, or "Katy") arrived in the area in 1893, building from Dallas and San Antonio to Houston. It bypassed the original town of Cat Spring about a mile and a half to the south; soon the entire town moved to a new location on the railroad, and grew from there to the present time.

The first school in the area was built in Cat Spring in 1842. Ferdinand Engelking described it to his mother in a letter dated January 8, 1843: "Deaths in Cat Spring have for a long time not

---

4  *Indian Papers of Texas and the Southwest*, edited by Dorman H. Winfrey and James M. Day, Vol. I, p. 50 (Austin, Texas State Historical Association, 1995)

been so frequent, and one hears of more births, and the young children grow healthy and strong. A schoolhouse was built the previous summer, and one looks for competent teachers, as the three oldest children are seven years old."[5]

In his 1899 Supplement to the Bellville Wochenblatt titled "A History of Austin County", William Trenckmann described Cat Spring as follows:

"Cat Spring lies southwest of Bellville and like Bellville, at the fringe of the post oak forest area. It is the second oldest German settlement in the county. In the year 1834 the Amsler brothers and soon thereafter the von Roeder family settled here on land grants that had been made to them by the Republic of Texas.

"To old Mr. M. Hartmann, who came into the country in 1847, we owe much interesting information about olden days. He makes the following report about the first settlers:

"Amsler too did not have his land surveyed until Louis von Roeder appeared as the 'Deus ex machina' with a big bag of Spanish doubloons. They made a trade that von Roeder was to survey the land and to receive a third of a league for his work.

"Mr. von Roeder built himself a home on what is now the Gloor place, next to the spring which was later called Cat Spring because a wild cat had been killed near it. "In order to complete it quickly, his sons went into the nearby woods, got poles as thick as an arm, set them into the ground two feet apart, nailed shingles on them and added a roof, a door, and a dormer window, also all made out of shingles. The interior was lined with clay and wood, and on the walls Mr. von Roeder pasted pictures from illustrated journals. When his sister, Mrs. von Ploeger, who had come from Germany in the meantime, stepped into this palace, she is said to have fainted from the shock.

"The fields of the young von Roeders were small, and from a distance looked as if the owners were cultivating cockle burrs.

---

[5] von Roeder F, Engelking S. *The Engelking Letters*. CreateSpace; 2012. Available as paperback or Kindle eBook format at www.amazon.com.

Their chief occupations seem to have been cattle raising, hunting, and fishing. When they had collected enough rawhides and pelts, these were sent by a passing teamster to Houston. In addition to their household necessities, the teamster was obligated to bring back a keg of whiskey. 'Then there was great Joy in Israel.' Drinking bouts were staged with much toasting in the manner of students in Germany. Whenever it was convenient, Ernst of Industry and his boon[6] companions attended these bouts. Then there was unbounded joviality with quite solemn duels and fights that often had rather disturbing consequences.

"When Mr. Hartmann came to Texas he found a friend of his youth in the bookbinder Jean Baptiste Dros, who had come to meet him in Houston. In Cat Spring he also found Flato, Hagemann, Bolten, Mersmann, Sens, Kinkler, Glaum, Dittert, Welhausen, Levermann, Hollien, Clarke, Sam and Frank Everett, Allen and others.

"Those were jolly days in old Cat Spring. The majority of the first settlers were lively young people of the educated class; however, their descendants and the later settlers to whom the practical side of life was more important, have preserved many of the attributes of their genial forebears. Hypocrisy and bad tempers flourish no better in present day Cat Spring than they did in olden times.

"Until long after the (Civil) war Cat Spring remained the strongest German settlement in the southern part of the county and the gathering place of the Germans. On the seventh of June, 1856, the first "Landwirt- Schaftliche Verein" (Agricultural Society) was founded here with A. F. Trenckmann as president and M. Hartmann as secretary. Worthy Germans from Cat Spring, Bellville, and the Bernard joined, and the carefully written minutes are eloquent witnesses of the serious aims and activities of the members. The society, which rendered great services to the progress of agriculture, exists today, with 230 members.

---

6   By "boon", the author probably is referring to the companions which fortune had brought together. The translator may be rendeing the German word *Segen* – a blessing.

"Soon after the war the Turnverein "Gut Heil" was organized here, and in the thirty years of its existence it has made a fine contribution to the social life of the community. This society owns a hand-some hall in Cat Spring.

"Today the population of the town is exclusively German and Bohemian. In 1892 the M.K.and T. Railroad built a depot a mile southwest of the business area of Old Cat Spring, and the post office and all the businesses were moved to the new location. The town now has two important general merchandise stores, two blacksmith shops, two saloons, a furniture store, a saddle shop, which also carries tinware, ironware and buggies, a lumberyard, a millinery shop, and two butcher shops. In the last eight months 2,316 bales of cotton were shipped by rail against 1,800 in the previous season. Cat Spring and the neighboring New Burg have good schools in which English and German are taught.

"Among the pioneers of Cat Spring who have lived there for fifty years or longer we can list M. Hartmann, Kasper Stuessel, Joachim and Jakob Koeding, Heinrich Siewert and wife, Heinrich Dethloff, Heinrich Waak and Fritz Eckelberg, all of whom are standing on the brink of eighty or have crossed it."

## Hermann University

The second institution of higher education in Texas was promoted by German settlers from Cat Spring, Industry and Frelsburg and was intended to be built at Cat Spring. Reutersville College was the first, chartered in 1840. In 1844 the German settlers of the Cat Spring/Industry/Frelsburg area, led by Friedrich Ernst and Rev. Louis Erdvenberg, appealed to the Congress of the Republic of Texas, who, on January 27, 1844, granted a franchise to the "Hermann University" which was to teach philosophy, medicine, theology and jurisprudence. A league of land was awarded to help finance the project. The professors were all to be able to lecture in both English and German. The theology professor was not to be affiliated with and particular religious denomination, nor teach any sect... The University was to be located either on Mill Creek or Cummins Creek, with Cat Spring as the intended target. The incorporators of Hermann University were L.C. Erdvenberg, F. Ernst, H. Schmidt, H. Amthor, J.G. Lieper, G. Stoehr, F.W. Huesmann and E. Franke. The university building was to be financed by sale of shares of stock at a par value of $50. This was a problem in that the German settlers had little cash, and the land they were able to pledge was of little use since they already had ample land with the Republic grant. Failure to sell the required shares of stock led to the annulment of the franchise by Congress in January of 1846. The franchise was renewed on April 11, 1846 with minor modifications, but the stock still did not sell and the project remained dormant for two decades.

The state legislature provided for reincorporation of the school on August 10, 1870, with shares to be sold at fifteen dollars and granted to the school a league in Gillespie County. Frelsburg, Colorado County, was selected for the location, and a two-story building was erected, but the university never opened. The act of incorporation was repealed on November 1, 1871. The property was sold to the Frelsburg public schools and became known as The Hermann Seminar. Millheim native William Andreas Trenckmann taught there briefly in 1879.

---

The *Austin County Times* newspaper, printed in Bellville, published a special edition on September 15, 1883, in which were given the history of the various towns then in existence in the county. The entry for Cat Spring follows:

**The Austin County Times**
**W.C. Hill, Editor and Proprietor**
**Saturday, September 15, 1883**

**TOWNS OF AUSTIN COUNTY**

**PIONEER PEOPLE**
Resumé of Early History of the Settlements
**WHERE THE WILD INDIAN ROVED**
The Men and Women Who Helped Make Texas What She is
**THE PAST AND PRESENT**
The Pioneers of Then and the Business Men of Now
Where to Get a Home
Climate, Soil, Timber, Prairie, Water, and Products
**FERTILE FIELDS AND FREE**
A Land That Will Laugh With a Harvest When it is Tickled With a Plow
**ALMOST A PARADISE HERE**
A Happy and Prosperous People Who Will Welcome New Neighbors

*Cat Spring*

Some time after the war for Texas independence had closed, there turned up about where Bellville now stands a young German. He had come to Texas to find some suitable employment and a home. He entered T.G. Bell's house and was kindly received. On learning what he wanted Mr. Bell told him if he followed the Coshatte trail until he crossed Mill Creek he would find a lot of his countrymen and be accommodated. Louis Leverman, (this was the young man's name) set out as directed, but he had the misfortune to lose the trail[7] in the creek bottom and wandered about that day, the next night and the following day, till towards evening, crossing the creek several times without being able to find his way out. At last he sat down in despair

---

7   This early road was blazed in 1805 by the Coushatta Indians who had just moved to Texas from Louisiana. They used it to travel to La Bahia (Goliad) to trade. It was used extensively by American settlers in the 1820s and 1830s. It crossed the Brazos at what became the Jared Groce Plantation south of modern Hempstead, Mill Creek at the modern Hwy. 2429 bridge, went past Elemenech Swearingen's house whee it intersected the Gotier trace, then crossed the Colorado at the Atascosito Crossing some eight miles below Columbus. See details at Jim Woodrick's Texas History Snippets at http://texashistorysnippets.blogspot.com.

and prepared to die with hunger and fatigue, when, lo, he heard the crowing of a cock in a southern direction. He was enlivened with new hope, and following the direction of the repeated crowing he reached the home of E. Swearingen at ... (text lost in original) ... hospitality of Mr. and Mrs. Swearingen soon brought the deeply sunken vital powers of the young man up, and after a few days rest he set his wandering foot out again in a westerly direction as directed by Mr. Swearingen. and soon found Mr. F. Swearingen, the father of E. Swearingen, and a little farther, C.C. Amsler, Louis von Roeder, of whose five sons and two daughters, Otto, Albrecht and Louis were married and each lived on a farm of his own. The eldest daughter was married to Louis Kleberg, and the youngest afterward married F. Engelking, now of Millheim. Further there were Robert and Ernst Kleberg, the latter unmarried. N.E. Clarke and A. Citz. Old Louis von Roeder died soon after, at the house of his son-in-law, Louis Kleberg, then county surveyor.

## *FOUNDATION*

C.C. Amsler had come to Texas as early as 1832. He had been granted by the Mexican government—which was very profuse in donating land to attract immigration—a league of land. When the war of independence broke out he left his young wife with a friend at Industry and went to fight the Mexicans till the close of the war. Land was again granted to him by the republic of Texas in payment for his services, and so he had plenty of land but not one cent to pay for its location and survey. Happily for him at this time Louis von Roeder made his appearance with doubloons, eagles, etc., to the amount of $8,000, a large sum of cash on hand at that time. I have heard several times that the island of Galveston was offered him for a trifle, but it seemed too dreary a place to be good for anything. Now with the help of some money from Louis von Roeder and the intelligence of his sons, who had a thorough education, Amsler succeeded in locating what is called the Louis von Roeder league and his other lands in the neighborhood, but he had to give to Louis von

Roeder one-third of the league. Now began a life of work and hardship and privation of these families for which they were ill-fitted. In Germany they belonged to the best classes, had moved there in high society and in the best circles, and their education was of a high order. They bore the change bravely. Their social and gatherings were highly attractive and much sought; their conversation moved on topics not in the reach of every one, and they were animated by wit and humor. Louis von Roeder had brought with him also a wagon, the first and only one then in the country, and his sons made trips with it, hauling goods for merchants, and on one of these trips from Houston they cleared $500. Truck-wheel wagons were in use then generally, and C.C. Amsler hauled his brother Marcus and family on such a wagon with two yoke of oxen from Houston to Cat Spring.

## *NAME*

Cat Spring was named after a never failing spring in its midst, on which the settlers were dependent for their water, and after a wild cat was seen near it. The year 1846 brought a good many immigrants to Cat Spring. John Hollien, also a soldier of the war of Independence, had gone to Germany and brought over a wife and her brother, F. Ramm and wife, and both had settled previously. Albrecht and Otto von Roeder and Robert Kleberg sold their estate to these newcomers and moved to Dewitt county. Robert Kleberg was afterwards elected county judge of that county; names of these newcomers were C. Welhousen, F. Lass, Jacob Kinkler, John Glaum, Chr. Dittert, C. Palm, and others. About 1850 H. Lange of Hamburg erected a saw mill, and F. Laas built a cotton gin and grist mill, but the former, after H. Lange's death, was transformed by Fedor Soder into a store, and the latter after having been transformed into a church by E. Bergmann, was blown down by a hurricane. After this C.C. Amsler built a cotton gin and grist mill driven by oxen, and later by steam. Franz Ray followed with another one of a smaller size. After the late (Civil) war we had a very valuable influx to our population by immigrants from Mecklenberg. They fled from a state of serfage there which is not quite extinct in that country. They brought scanty means, but by their thrift, energy and economy they were soon able to buy school lands, on which they have now comfortable homes. Many of them are even well off and among our best citizens. A few years ago they built, with great exertion and sacrifice, a schoolhouse where their children are instructed and a home for the teacher. About this time it was it when Hassler & Kinkler and Charles and Henry Langhammer started their stores and when C.C. Amsler sold his place to F. Schlapuder and moved to Spring creek.

### *PRESENT CONDITION*

Cat Spring now has three stores, owned by H. Langhammer, Hassler & Kinkler and Peters and Soloman, all of which are doing a good business; a first class steam cotton gin, grist mill, saw mill and planing machine, Franz Schlapuder, proprietor; a horse-powered cotton gin and grist mill, Joach. Bade, proprietor; a blacksmith, tin, and wagon shop, E. ... (text lost in original) ... postoffice, F. Peters, postmaster; saddler shop, H. Hess; two barrooms, and two shoe shops; Dr. Williamson, physician; a public free school, Theo. Meyer, teacher. Cat Spring has an agriculture society founded in 1856, the oldest in the state, with more than 100 members. It has monthly meetings, and is in correspondence with the agriculture department at Washington and the signal office, and receives from the former very valuable reports, seeds, plants, etc. every year. The officers are: Chas. Sens, president; H.A. Hartmann, secretary; H. Langhammer, treasurer. It also has a turnsverein, with a splendid hall and grounds, which are used for social amusements, festivals, etc. The officers are: A. Malecheck, president; M. Hartmann, secretary; Fr. Kroener, treasurer.

---

The Houston Post issue of Sunday, May 19, 1936 ran a special article in Section 4, page 6, that told the Cat Spring story. While full of embellishment and factual errors, the story nevertheless conveys the spirit of the community.

**Germans Who Fled Early Iron Rule Prosper at Cat Spring**
**WILDCAT SPRING IN 1831 ... TAME AS A HOUSE CAT NOW**
Wildcat Chases By Youngsters of Village Old Sport
Gay Spot of County Seat In 1832 Was Big Saloon
Tales of Interest About Settlers Abound in Area
Wearing of Hats and Spurs Forbidden in Hall.
by H.H. Edge Post Farm Editor

*Caption under three images:*

One hundred and five years ago, this free-flowing spring, shown in the center picture, was shared with wildcats by early settlers and the town, now known as Cat Spring in Austin county where many notable Texas figures were born, was called Wildcat Spring. Charles Dittert, one of the pioneers who farms in this community, is shown dipping water from the old spring as Oscar Zeiske, who chased wildcats in the early days with hounds, looks on. Dittert, a rugged German and descendant of a cultured Prussian family, is shown standing at the right. His brother, Chas. Dittert, the village blacksmith for 40 years and president of the Cat Spring Agricultural society, the oldest in Texas, is shown at the left with a wagon wheel he is finishing for a farmer customer. The von Roeder family received the grant on which this old spring is located, from Stephen F. Austin and the town that grew up was named after the wildcats that infested the woods and insisted on using the spring as their fountain. The spring is about 20 miles west of San Felipe, the cradle of Texas liberty, and such Texas pioneers as Robert J. Kleberg, grandfather of Richard Kleberg, Texas congressman, settled at Wildcat Spring. It is now one of the most interesting and progressive agricultural communities in Texas where a program of sound diversified farming has been carried on for over a century.

## *Cat Spring, May 9*

A wildcat crouched on its haunches at the base of an old oak tree and wet its whiskers in the bubbling waters from which Valeska von Roeder had hung out the family washing the night before. It was in early 1832. Louis, Albrecht and Valeska, children of Ludwig von Roeder of Prussia had camped 20 miles west of San Felipe de Austin, the cradle of Texas liberty. They were seeking personal, religious and political liberty and freedom, from the tyrannies abounding in their native country.

Near an ever-flowing stream between Mill creek and Cummings creek, the von Roeders had been given a grant in the Stephen F. Austin colony.

The first night strange cries rent the air, and the following morning wildcats were beating a path to and from the spring and the site was immediately named "Katzenquelle". Later it was changed to Wildcat Spring.

In the 104 years that have followed the woods and fields have been tamed and this is just Cat Spring, a village of 316 industrious people who live off the land and are descendants of a handful of Germans who fled the oppressions of early monarchies.

## *Settled by Kleberg*

Here, where wildcats were in abundance for several years, settled Robert Kleberg, grandfather of Richard Kleberg, a Texas congressman; E.G. Maetze, a former United States senator from Texas, and Charles Nagel, a former U.S. secretary of labor who now lives in St. Louis at the age of 84 years.

Men of 60 year to 70 who now live in Bellville, the county seat of Austin county, including R.E. and Oscar Zeiske, weekly newspaper publishers, tell exciting stories of the wildcats from Wildcat Spring.

For instance, wildcats were just like kittens to Fritz Mersmann, and old-timer of Austin county and Wildcat Spring was a paradise to him.

Once a week Mersmann caught the wildest wildcat he could corner and hauled it by buggy to Bellville where the kitty was sold to the Bellville young-bloods whose principle sport was chasing wildcats with their packs of hounds.

The gay spot of the county seat in those days was the Schauer-Hammer and Roensch saloon and when Mersmann caught a wildcat he took it to this bar where it was kept in a cage overnight.

One morning when Sol Jackson, the negro saloon porter, opened the doors, a wildcat was ready to spring from a keg of ale behind the bar. It had escaped the cage.

Oscar Zeiske said it took two rope hands and a half day to corner the beast and lasso it in the cellar of the saloon while a score of the natives suffered from the lack of the usual eye-opener. A striking note in the evidence of the culture of these early Texas settlers is seen in an 8-year-old sign that has a place in the community hall of Cat Spring. It reads:

"Wearing of hats or spurs and chewing or smoking are strictly forbidden in this hall.".

## *Spurs Are Barred*

This was forbidden, according to Charles Dittert, a pioneer farmer of the section, out of respect for the women and girls and spurs were barred because of the hazard to the wide swishing dresses of their wives and daughters. The sign is still posted in the hall that is controlled by the "Landwirtschaftliche Verein," the oldest agricultural society in Texas.

[Ed. note: this sign still exists and is hung on the wall of the agricultural society hall. Shown below, it says "The wearing of hats and spurs, and smoking and chewing (tobacco) in this hall is forbidden.]

The eightieth anniversary of this society will be celebrated next June 7 at the hall, located on a hill just east of the old wildcat spring which continues to flow cool, clear water from the bottom of another hillside.

Cat Spring abounds in historical interest. Recently Arthur L. Schuette, principal of the local school, and his advanced pupils, have collaborated in compiling data that abounds in romance and the excitement which resulted in the naming of this town.

In a synopsis of the material collected by his pupils and Schuette, wildcats inspired the name.

The narrative tells that, on April 3, 1831, Friedrich Ernst and his family landed at San Felipe. This was the first German family settling in Texas. Other Germans came to Texas principally through the informations gained from a letter written by Ernst, the founder of the town of Industry, to his friends in Grossherzogtum Oldenburg. In 1832, Louis, Albrecht, Joachim and their sister Valeska von Roeder, the children of Lieutenant Lugwig von Roeder, came to Texas to live under a free republican form of government.

These people, according to the story, were of the finest German blood and blazed the trail for other German immigrants. The Von Roeders decided to locate about 20 miles west of San Felipe an a land grant deeded to them as colonists of Stephen F. Austin. It is here, approximately in the center of the first Austin colony, that they settled.

Although there are several versions of how Cat Spring got its name, it seems to be authentic that it derived its name from the fact that the woods surrounding the spring were full of wildcats. Pioneers had no set rules in selecting names for towns. In this case, it seems that, when the Von Roeders camped the first night on their grant, the wildcats kept them awake and early in the morning monopolized the spring.

## *Water Power Mill*

When other German settlers came, Louis von Roeder erected a water power mill and the place became known for a while as "Roedermill." In later years it was Wildcat Spring, until 1834 when Robert Kleberg built the first store it became Cat Spring. Soon a log church, a dance hall by Marcus Amsler and an Inn by Charles Amsler were constructed. It then became a little Germany, the center of German culture and refinement, a center which to this day has preserved the typical German mind and character and from which German immigrants radiated to various parts of Texas.

For those immigrants — German or Anglo-Saxon — who landed at San Felipe and who wanted to go to other settlements west from here, it became a landmark and refuge of peace and happiness of pioneer days.

Soon here were found such families as the Klebergs, Amslers, Trenckmanns, Kloss, Amtors, Bergmann, Maetze, Nagel and Dittert.

San Felipe was the nearest post office. Mail came once a month. The settlers got their mail from J.H. Bostick, who had settled as one of the Austin colonists in 1827 about 10 miles north from Cat Spring, on Mill creek. Fritz Peters was the first unofficial postmaster for Cat Spring from 1848 to 1853, when the United States government made Charles Amsler the first official postmaster. Before and during the Civil war, a Mr. Strauss was the mail carrier between San Felipe and La Grange.

These German settlers soon forgot their noble birth, and set to work with characteristic thoroughness to develop their adopted country. In an attempt to make progress in a co-operative way, A.F. Trenckmann and others called a meeting to discuss the feasibility of forming some sort of an organization for the development of agriculture.

Forty farmers responded to this call, and they met in the log church, where they organized the "Landwirtschaftliche Verein," or agricultural society, the oldest in Texas. It was organized on June 7, 1856, and is still in existence, with Chris Dittert, for 40 years a blacksmith of Cat Spring, the president.

A desire to establish a means of education was not lacking among these German refugees, because illiteracy was considered a stigma to their social standing. Those who could afford it hired private tutors and others taught their own.

One of the amusing features of early education was that "Emilie," a book written by Rousseau, became the basis for character building. When, in 1840, the settlers discussed the feasibility of establishing a university - Herman university — it found favor not only among the Germans, but also among the Anglo-Saxons. Even the Sam Houston administration looked favorably on this project, which, at that time, seemed utopian. In 1843 the congress of the republic ordered ordered a university to be established between Mill creek and Cummings creek. It was then that A. F. Trenckmann, the Rev. Bergmann and Robert J. Kleberg and others planned to build the institution at Cat Spring. Lack of finances prevented the scheme from materializing.

## Charter Cancelled

On January 27, 1844, the Texas congress granted a charter to E.J. Ervendberg, F. Ernst, H. Amthor and others. This charter was cancelled when these men could not raise the necessary funds. It was renewed on April 11, 1846, and H. Amthor, E. Franke, H. Draub, H. Ernst, Jacob Rein, E. Miller, E.H. Yordt, Dr. E. Becker and Herman Frels became trustees. They succeeded in erecting a building at Frelsburg, a German settlement about 20 miles west of Cat Spring. It was not a success. In later years it became known as Herman seminary, and was used for a public school until 1926, when it was destroyed by fire.

The plan of establishing a higher institution of learning at this stage of the development of Texas was considered by many as premature and impractical. The state then had but a few students, as there were no schools to prepare students for college or university.

In writing about this phase of the development of the state, Schuette writes:

"This attempt was however, a ray of light passing fleetingly through an opening of the passing cloud of darkness, and showed that beyond the horizon there was intelligence and civilization, which was gradually pushing primitiveness away. Not lacking courage and fortitude, in spite of their failure to establish an institution of higher education, the German settlers in and around Cat Spring, under the leadership of the Rev. Bergman, opened up a private school in a log church which was located on the hill near Kollatschney cemetery, while Ernest Gustav Maetze opened a private school at nearby Mulheim. "Thus, in the time of peace and war, the funders of our little village, Cat Spring had not failed to render aid to their newly adopted country. In time of peace they developed and cleared the wilderness and made it safe for human habitation; they rendered aid to the government in enforcing laws and built up schools which became the centers in perpetuating their ideals and culture. In time of war they shouldered their weapons of defense and helped protect the frontier against Indian depredations and to preserve the liberty of Texas.

"Among the outstanding characters who took part in the war of independence are Charles Amsler, a native of Switzerland, who emigrated to Texas and settled at Cat Spring in 1834 and took part in the storming of San Antonio under Ben Milam, and the Von Roeders and Robert Kleberg, who were members of Baker's company."

One of the most important factors in the development of this entire region, according to Charles Dittert, an early-day farmer, has been the agricultural society.

### *Scientific Farming*

From the very first, 80 years ago, this society has encouraged diversified and scientific farming. Various members, from time to time, have been assigned to make researches into improved phases of agriculture and transmitting their findings to the members of the society. This community reflects a high standard of agriculture and thrift particular to the German-settled sections of the state.

So much interest has developed in recent months in the motives back of the influx of some 10,000 German settlers into Texas, es-

# Cat Spring

pecially during the period of 1844 - 1850, the revolutionary period there, that Dr. R.L. Biesele, associate professor of history at the University of Texas, has been granted a leave of absence for the spring semester from his teaching duties to permit him to spend full time in research.

He has been working on a survey of this german colonization movement for several years from the university bureau of research in the social sciences.

Through Dr. Biesele's efforts, transcripts have been made of a vast quantity of materials of which originals are in German libraries but of which photostats have been made for the library of congress. There are some 70 volumes of these transcripts. The originals are known as the Solms-Braunfels archives. It is this material which Dr. Biesele now proposes to study and digest in an effort to make comprehensive the survey of the backgrounds of the Solms-Braunfels colonization project.

Unlike the educated and cultured who first settled at Cat Spring, the German colonists who came to Texas as a result of this later immigration scheme mainly were peasants who felt the need of economic freedom that was lacking in their own country, Dr. Biesele explains, On the other hand, leaders of the project were noblemen who stressed the philanthropic aspect of the undertaking but whose motives were undoubtably tinged with mercenary considerations, he declares.

Under the terms of the grant which the Society for the Protection of German Immigrants to Texas and with Fisher and Miller, impresarios, each German colonist who was married received 640 acres of land and each single man over 17 years of age received 320 acres. The society received half these amounts respectively for each settler it brought in, plus a premium of 10 sections of land for each 100 married man and five sections for each 100 single men, on condition that it brought to Texas 6000 families or families and single men by March, 1848.

Descendants of these 10,000 German immigrants still remain to form a not inconsiderable element in the Texas melting pot of nationalities. It is significant, however, that of the noblemen leaders of the immigration project, only one actually came to Texas and settled here.

This was Baron Ottfried Hans von Meusbach, who became second commissioner general of the Society for the Protection of German Immigrants in Texas and was founder of Fredericksburg.

*Quotes from Book*

In his book, "The History of the German Settlement in Texas," published some years ago. Dr. Biesele said of von Meusbach: "Baron Ottfried Hans von Meusbach. known in Texas by the name of John O. Meusbach, under which he was a naturalized citizen of Texas and the United States, was born in Dillenburg, Nassau, on May 12, 1812, where his father held the position of solicitor. "Meusbach studied mining and natural science at the academy of mining and forestry in Clausthal in the Herz mountains. At the universities of Bonn and Halle he studied law, political economy and finance. For a while, he served the Prussian government as an official connected with the supreme court of justice at Naumberg and Stettin, after which he held an administrative position at Stettin. The royal government at Stettin sent him as commissioner in Anciamatti to bring order into the communal affairs of that place. On February 24, 1845, he was appointed to succeed Prince Solms as commissioner general of the society in Texas.

"During his tenure in this position he founded Fredericksburg, Castell and Leiningen and made a treaty with the Comanche Indians. On July 20, 1847, he was succeeded by Herman Spiess. In 1851 he was elected state senator for the district comprising Bexar, Medina and Comal and on September 28, 1852, he married Agnes, the Countess of Coerth. Two years later, Governor Pease appointed him commissioner for the colony of the German Immigration company, in which capacity he issued land certificates to the immigrants brought to Texas by the German society.

"For a while he farmed at Comanche Springs in Bexar county, where he was also justice of the peace. Then he moved to Waco Springs on the Guadalupe, a few miles above New Braunfels. After living in Fredericksburg for a few years, he moved to his farm halfway between Fredericksburg and Mason and laid out the town of Loyal Valley, where he held several public offices. On May 27, 1897, he died at Loyal Valley, one of the noted pioneers of the Republic of Texas."

There is a similar background to the early settlers of Cat Spring and that of Robert J. Kleberg is typical.

When the Kleberg family landed at Harrisburg, a full library and a piano were among the effects. All of this was destroyed in the fire in 1834, following which they moved to Cat Spring.

This grandfather of the present Texas congressman was a doctor of law on the facility of the University of Goettingen in Prussia and he, with his Cat Spring neighbors, aided materially in the establishment of higher institutions of learning in Texas.

Thus, as San Felipe became the center of Anglo-Saxon culture and refinement in Texas, Cat Spring, once a nest of wildcats, settled by the Teutonic race, became a center of spreading the ideals that reach into more than a score of German colonies all over the state.

# Letters That Sparked German and Czech Emmigration

Texas was truly a land of opportunity. Within a decade after Stephen Austin began his American colonization efforts in Mexican Texas, the first German family arrived and settled in 1831 at what became Industry. Friedrich Ernst was the patriarch of this pioneer family, and soon wrote a lengthy letter back to Germany extolling the virtues of his new home and inviting his friends to join him. His letter received wide circulation, and in short order more Germans were leaving for Texas. Among the first of these was the extended family of Ludwig Anton Siegmund von Roeder, who settled what became Cat Spring. Many thousands of German immigrants followed in the ensuing decades. Ernst is remembered as the person singly most responsible for the starting large scale German immigration to Texas.

Two decades later the first family of Czechs came to Texas and settled in Cat Spring. Josef Arnošt Bergmann, a Lutheran preacher, arrived with his family in 1849 and like Ernst before him, promptly wrote a letter back to his friends describing his new home in glowing terms. His letter was published in Czech newspapers and became the springboard for large group migrations of Czechs to Texas. Many of these early Czech arrivals settled in the Cat Spring / Industry area, including Joseph Lidumil Leshikar, the primary organizer of the first two groups to arrive in 1851 and 1853.

Both the Ernst and Bergmann letters are included herein, due to their connection to Cat Spring, and to their huge importance in setting the stage for hundreds of thousands of German- and Czech-Texans today.

# Friedrich Ernst Letter, undated but probably early 1832

From a Settlement on Mill Creek in Austin's Colony in the state of Texas in New Mexico.

In keeping with my request, the travel account that I sent to my brother-in-law right after our arrival in New York will have been shared with all of you. It contained everything that I considered necessary to report. At that time I had nothing to say about America, but now that I have spent more than two years on this continent and so far have traveled more than 1,400 miles across it, I can at least tell you what should be especially useful to emigrants; these few sheets of writing paper do not allow room for more, and even so I shall have to be brief, so without further ado, I'll set out right away. It will be mentioned only in passing that we went by way of Munster, Wesel, Maastricht, Brussels, Ostend, Dunkirk, Abbeville, and Dieppe to Havre-de-Grace, and from there crossed the Atlantic Ocean on a packet ship to New York within four weeks, and reached this immeasurable city with its two hundred thousand inhabitants. However, in the north the United States does not offer immigrants its former advantages. Here we found winter to be just as severe as in Germany, for which reason we decided to go farther south. Accordingly, we took ship in February and went to New Orleans on a brig. Even though it was severe winter right at our departure from New York, nevertheless on the fourth day after our leave the mild air of spring was already wafting toward us, and three days later, between Cuba and Florida, we had veritable summer, which persisted the entire distance of one thousand nautical miles across that part of the ocean, through the Bahama Bay into the Gulf of Mexico, right to the mouth of the Mississippi. Our brig was towed 120 miles up to New Orleans by a steamship, which already had two brigs and one schooner in tow. In New Orleans we received favorable reports about Texas and Austin's Colony located there, so we took passage on a thirty-seven-ton schooner, the Satillo, which already had more than one hundred people on board, and after a week-long trip landed at Harrisburg in this colony. Every immigrant who wants to farm receives a league of land if he arrives with wife or family, or if as a single man, a quarter- league; sons over fourteen years of age have identical claims on land distribution. A league is an hour's journey long and just as wide; in return he must defray 160 dollars in regular payments for surveyor's fees, installation costs, etc., must take the oath of citizenship, and after the course of a year is a free citizen of the free United States of Mexico. As Europeans who are especially welcome, we, too, received a league of land in this same manner and settled there; that is where I'm writing this letter from. The state [province] of Texas, of which our colony constitutes almost one-sixth, is located to the south, on the Gulf of Mexico, between the 27th and the 31st northern latitude; previously followers of Napoleon had settled here at Camp d'Asile. Austin's Colony is traversed by the Trinidad, Rio Brazos, and Rio Colorado rivers; within it are situated the major seat of St. Felippe de Austin and the townships of Harrisburg, Brazoria, and Matagorda. Tampico and Vera Cruz can be reached by sail in three to four days. The land is undulating and alternates between woodlands and expanses of native grass. They are showy with the most wonderful flowers and blossoms, such as magnolias. The meadows have the most sumptuous stands of grass; I should have been able to sell several thousand cartloads of hay, if there had only been takers; but instead of being mowed it is burned off in late summer.

The soil is so rich it never requires fertilizing. The climate resembles that of lower Italy; during the summer it is admittedly warmer than in Germany, because we have the sun almost directly overhead. On the other hand, it is not nearly as hot as might be presumed, since a persistent fresh east breeze cools the air; moreover, in the summertime there is not much to do, and people wear light clothing such as white cotton trousers and vests. In winter, like right now, the weather is usually what Germany has during the first two weeks of spring in March. Only twice so far, when the wind was blowing hard from the northwest, have we had freezing ice. In an entire month the weather will prevent fieldwork only for a couple of days. The sun and air are always bright and clear; bees and butterflies are seen year round, birds are singing in the shrubs, some of which are evergreen; and in winter as well as in summer the cattle find their own feed. The cows calve without assistance and come home at night to suckle their calves, which are kept in the daytime in an area protected by a wooden fence. In this way the return of the cows is assured. Calves are never slaughtered. A cow with calf costs ten dollars. There are one hundred cents to a dollar, so a cent is about equal to an Oldenburg Grote. Horses cost somewhat more and are only used for riding; everybody rides, whether male or female. Oxen are used for draft animals and plowing. There are farmers here who own close to seven hundred head of cattle. But the rate of propagation is also quite extraordinary, and young cows of 1¾ years of age already bring calves into the world. Hogs increase so astonishingly that, beginning with six, you may have one hundred the following year; they, too, cost nothing to maintain, since they find abundant feed in the woods and only occasionally are given a few kernels of corn to get them used to the house. Moreover, pork is at a good price with four dollars per hundred pounds. A local immigrant bought six sows two years ago; after breeding them he has now sold eighty fat hogs, each one of them over two hundred pounds. Generally speaking, all agricultural products fetch a good price greatly to the farmer's advantage. Corn, or Turkish wheat, costs seventy-five cents to a dollar per bushel and is as good as cash money—of which there is not much in circulation, since everything is transacted by barter. On one Morgen of good land, which can be plowed in one day, thirty to forty bushels of corn will grow, for which the seed corn can be planted by children. Fields for planting are protected by split wooden enclosures so the cattle won't ruin anything, since they are allowed to run at large. The products cultivated here consist of sugarcane, cotton of best quality, tobacco, rice, indigo—which grows wild around here—corn, batatas or sweet potatoes, melons of exceptional quality, watermelons, pumpkins, wheat, rye, all kinds of garden vegetables, and peaches in great quantity. Moreover, growing wild in the woods are mulberries, several kinds of walnut, persimmons as sweet as honey, and grapes in large quantity but not of outstanding taste. Honey is frequently found in hollow tree trunks, where bee swarms settle; there are birds of all kinds, from pelicans to hummingbirds, and game such as deer, bears, raccoons, opossum, wild turkeys, geese, ducks, and partridges—these last-mentioned are in quantity and as large as domestic chickens; they are actually gray pheasants. From our house in particular, we daily see flocks of game grazing. Moreover, there is free hunting every where, and very delicate fish, sometimes weighing forty pounds. There are also herds of foxes as well as of wild horses, which can be captured as colts and tamed. There are also wolves here, but of such a timid sort that they flee from my youngest children. Although a panther or leopard (cougar or ocelot) may be seen from time to time, predators are, generally speaking, not dangerous. I have wandered for days alone in the deepest thicket, where no human had set foot before, without ever seeing any such animal; on the other hand, the hunting bounty is always great and provides us with the most exquisite roasts. The meadows are adorned with the most beautiful, gorgeous flowers, some of which I never saw before, and which in Germany can only be grown in a greenhouse; I feel ashamed to scatter the seeds brought from home where the carpet of meadowland displays a continuous show of flowers. There are also many kinds of snakes here, among them the rattlesnake, several of which I have killed. How little they are noticed is proved by the fact that many a hunter or herdsman walks barefoot all summer long, through all kinds of tall grass and brush, without even thinking of snakes. Furthermore, everybody knows remedies for the bites of such animals; three times I have seen people bitten, but never anyone die from it. In view of the large landholdings, it is obvious that the inhabitants cannot be living closely together; nevertheless my closest neighbor lives only ten minutes from my house, since we both have settled not far from our property line. A league of land comprises 4,444 acres or Morgen, consisting of hilly areas and valleys, woods and meadows cut through by small creeks, and when there are several settlements in one location the value of land is such that acreage has already been sold at one dollar. As in the United States the constitution of this country is free, and political quarrels are unknown to us here; still, by way of a newspaper regularly published at San Antonio on the Rio del Norte, we are informed of every world event. The English language is quickly learned; my wife and I, and my children in particular, can already manage fairly well, and I read the newspaper as well as I do a German one. Although the introduction of slaves is prohibited, keeping them is tacitly tolerated since there would otherwise be a shortage of laborers, because of it being so easy to earn a living. Working men earn seventy-five cents to a dollar a day with board. All items of clothing and footwear are expensive, so almost every one makes his own. In general, everybody lives in the open and by himself, so there is little need for cash money; thus I am quite happy finally to have my wishes fulfilled and find myself in a position where I can do everything according to my preferences. Everybody builds his own house, either by himself or with help from his neighbors; not much is spent on its beauty, rather it is only constructed of hewn wooden logs. Mine was built—with the assistance of my son Fritz, who can already cut down tree trunks two feet thick—on the order of my former garden house in Oldenburg, but on a larger scale. Working regularly in the open has made me healthier and stronger than I ever was in Germany, and my wife is blooming like a rose, as are the children. My son Hermann is growing exceptionally and turning into a genuine Mexican. They all have their rustic chores: Lina already milks her three cows, Fritz and Louis help me with farming, and the younger ones have various jobs such as planting and picking cotton, which is exceedingly easy since it grows like weeds. Every day fresh cornbread is made in an iron pot with a fireproof lid, and it tastes like the finest rice cakes. Our corn is of far better quality than in Germany; I grind it in a very simple manner and it yields not only meal but also shelled groats, like rice. Meat, which, from every kind of animal, is much tastier than in Germany, is eaten fried in the morning at breakfast, as well as at noon and in the evening. There are mosquitoes here just as in all warmer regions. Those who have been bitten by gnats on the German moors will consider this American nuisance worse over there than here. They are more frequent on the coast, but since we are living more than one hundred miles inland, where it is hillier and airier, we have little of this. In general I have no feeling of disadvantage except the great distance from my friends; if I could conjure them up, I would have heaven on earth. From the faithful description above, you will realize what advantages the farmer here has over the farmer over there; a free constitution and, for the time being, no local taxes whatever and later only slight ones; easy cattle raising, hardly three months of real work, no fertilizing of the acreage, no gathering of winter feed, no need for money, easy construction of houses and making of clothes, etc.; free hunting and game aplenty; everywhere free exercise of religion, etc.; all of this—with the best market for his products—combines to make the farmer happy and, in a few years, affluent. This is proved by everybody who has been here for four to six years. Up higher on the rivers there are beautiful areas, and silver has been found there; it is merely a matter of driving off an Indian tribe that resists individual visits. Several Indian tribes are moving about peacefully like Cossacks, hunting deer, of which they sell the hides. If some of you, my friends, or anybody else should decide, after reading this letter, to enjoy undisturbed freedom here and head for an assured pleasant future—instead of waiting until those few tangible possessions that remain vanish completely and thus being deprived of the means for passage—then let me offer the following advice with regard to the journey: book passage in steerage on one of the ships plying from the Weser River to New Orleans. I do not know the fare exactly, but it should not exceed forty-five dollars per person, since it would then be preferable to go to New York (costs thirty-five dollars and from there to New Orleans ten dollars, personal belongings free). From New Orleans to Texas (Harrisburg) ten dollars. Belongings are paid separately. Families should try for a discount; children usually pay half fare. You buy your own provisions. If the wind is favorable, the trip to New Orleans can be made in five to six weeks, and from there to Harrisburg in four days. Take passage so that you don't arrive in New Orleans between July and October, since yellow fever is prevalent there at that time. Once in Harrisburg, hire a wagon for San Felipe and report at the land office. It is safest to travel with several others, with one of them knowing the English language or studying it up to the time of departure. Each one must help the others, and if any of you only brings enough money to manage the very essential initial purchases, then what another among you may be paying beyond his share can soon be equalized. The head of a family must keep well in mind that the league of land granted him amounts to receiving as much land as a noble count owns, with an immediate value of six hundred to eight hundred dollars, at which price leagues have often been sold here already. Incidentally, the expenses for the land do not have to be paid immediately, and may be paid in cattle, which they raise themselves here. For my friends and other known countrymen I have, for the moment, enough room on my property, until they have the leisure to look for an unoccupied league, which does take time; however. Colonel Austin recently promised that such Germans as might arrive are to be well situated. An unmarried man should bring a woman who is not swayed by external appearances and what is fashionable. You, my dear C., have already experienced many setbacks in the world, which may cause you to wish for all memories to be erased. So, if there is any way to make this possible, do not delay for a moment coming over here with your loved ones; your brother, Hermann, who understands agriculture so thoroughly, would quickly be in his true element here. However, for professional people there is no particular prospect here. Bring your sisters; young girls can very well find their happiness here. If everybody comes whom I used to call a friend, nobody will lose anything by the exchange; next summer I will be building a house for prospective arrivals and will grow some fruit. May I soon have the pleasure of both being used quite shortly by friends; how happy that would make me. I expect no reply to this letter; communication from here is too difficult and uncertain. Come yourself and bring me letters from those who stayed behind; that would be the greatest joy for me. Once arrived in San Felipe, any of you should inquire about Friedrich Ernst on Mill Creek. Passports are nowhere required. My wife begs of your wife not to be afraid of the ocean voyage; at first she was so fearful she wouldn't go on board, but now that she has made two ocean voyages with me, she would surely travel with me around the world. Apart from a few gales, we didn't have a single misfortune and were barely seasick. Next August, when somebody from over there may possibly show up, our hopes will be stirring, and we shall believe it will be dear friends whenever a wagon arrives. Although the ocean and unanticipated bitter events separate us, I have still never ceased to be moved when I think of you, my dear friends, and you live daily in my heart.

Your Fritz[8]

---

8   This complete Ernst letter was copied with permission from the book *Journey to Texas* 1833, by Detlef Dunt translated by Anders Saustrup, edited and annotated by James C. Kearney and Gier Bentzen (Austin, University of Texas Press, 2015).

# Josef Arnošt Bergmann Letter, April 11, 1850

11 April 1850

Dear Friends, brothers and sisters:

In the end, it has taken a half-year for the trip from the time we left Strausney until our arrival. You have already heard how long we had to wait in Hamburg for a ship and that on 21 December before the Christmas holiday we were finally able to sail. Our ship Alexander was pretty and well built, and her captain skilled as a sailor and very friendly and good to us. Our quarters on the upper deck were adequate and habitable; our fellow travelers between the lower decks, however, were in bad conditions.

The ship, with space for 150 passengers, was half full from the start of the voyage. We spent our Christmas holidays on a calm ocean, though there was a great storm on Ash Wednesday. A strong wind started on Tuesday and this developed large waves and swells on Wednesday; Thursday and Friday it stormed without stopping and we did not see the sun in the daytime nor the stars at night - and even the captain was concerned. The conditions were scary and it was noticed how the mood of the people changed as they prepared to withstand the large swells and stormy winds. My greatest concern in all this rough weather was for the women and children who, in their sickness, could not hold themselves in their bunks and were afraid of being thrown out of their beds.

I and my family were not bad sick and other passengers did not understand how I could help my close friends and serve them in their sickness. I spent much time on deck holding to the railing and spent hours looking about and wondering about life during the storm. What I saw and felt then, I cannot describe in writing to anyone who has not experienced this situation. The ocean calmed down Sunday at 4:30 and after a refreshing nap, we were happy to learn we were between England and France. The sun came out and on one side, we saw the cliffs of England and on the other side the blue waters toward France.

On 31 December 1849, we stopped at the English port of Portsmouth so the ship could take on more passengers who awaited us here. On New Year's, I held services and gave thanks to the Lord for having protected us during the storm in which, I later learned, two ships (English and American) were shipwrecked. Calmness came after the winds and the children played happily on deck where we warmed ourselves in the sun. While our ship was at the dock, I looked around to see what was in the town and saw mainly the English ships which were as large as our homes and castles, and I wondered how the ocean can "push" them around.

Sunday after the New Year, we were furbished with fresh water and meat and sailed on. Our deck was normal and a happy one until we encountered the large waves and swells of the ocean; then most became seasick except the sailors; they had to vomit and their heads began to hurt so that they could hardly stay on their feet - but this sickness is not lasting or dangerous. Our food was not tasteful, perhaps because of the seasickness, and consisted of: dried peas three times a week, beans one day, rice once and once or twice we had rolls; then pork twice per week and salted beef on other days. In the morning we had black coffee and green tea at night with cookies made from wheat flour and without yeast; baked kolache twice a week but so hard that they were suitable only for good teeth, although quite tasteful with butter brushed on. At the end, we were served kraut and potatoes in lieu of the dried peas and rice - and this tasted better. In addition, one received a half-pound of butter, a half pound of sugar, and on Sunday a bottle of wine! Then it began to get warmer.

On 16 January 1850, there came a warm rain as would come to you on St. Johns.

On 17 January 1850, the sun came out at 6:45 and it was so bright and clear that one wondered - because never does the sun shine this brightly in Europe. Every day I waited for the sunrise on deck just so I could get a view of this beautiful sun. We had warm temperatures of 20 - 24 degrees Celsius.

On 25 January 1850, we arrived at the sign of the Crab and found hot temperatures of 20 - 24 deg. C. Here I saw, for the first time, the aurora borealis. The moon and the stars have an unusual appearance here and the nights are so different that a person stands for long hours and contemplates.

26 January 1850: We reached the half way mark on our road to America! Our route now takes us more northerly and then we will go to the south. The winds started to blow and in 24 hours we traveled forty to fifty miles of our journey; the mornings and nights were pretty - but the noon is sultry. Whales are seen daily and they come even to the ship and think nothing about the three guns that were fired into their midst. They are a strange animal and spray water through their noses which looks very pretty. There are other smaller fish, especially porpoises (dolphins) which are so numerous that we hardly noticed them. European birds have long left us so we see only the fish.

6 February 1850: The ocean was covered with a green moss (Saragasso Sea) and we pulled some of it aboard the ship. We saw it had white bulbs, something smaller than garlic or onions, and these are salty.

8 February 1850: We saw the Island of Haiti for the first land! Ach, even I cannot write of our gladness because for a long time we saw only the ocean and the heavens, and here we again see beautiful blue mountains and forests.

9 February, Saturday: The hog was killed and we picked our way further by the Islands of Haiti and Cuba - and for the occasion, on Sunday, we ate the whole hog! Tuesday, the ship was aimed toward the north so that the Island of Cuba was left to

the side. American birds began to fly around the ship. We suffered from the heat now and the captain let us prepare for a bath which enlivened myself and others.

23 February 1850: We saw America but it was so foggy that we had to stop.

27 February 1850: Wednesday at 6:00 in the night, we arrived offshore at Galveston and anchored close to the town.

1 March 1850: On Friday, our Captain went ashore.

2 March 1850: At 3:00 in the afternoon, we left our ship Alexander and rode a small American tug into Galveston where, at 6:00 in the night, we stepped for the first time on American land (soil). We lodged at a small German hotel "At the Stars".

4 March 1850: On Tuesday, I found a place to stay in another home because in the hotel we were required to pay one-half dollar per day per person (about one "zlaty" silver). So we lived on the boat from 20 January 1849 until 2 March 1850 and from the 6th of January to the 8th of February, we saw nothing other than the heavens and the ocean!

Galveston, a town in Texas, counts about a 5000 population and all homes, save the church and the Bureau (Federal Building) are built of wood and covered with oil paint for in such a warm climate other types of dwellings are not needed.

On our arrival, the potatoes were just in bloom and the gardens had English peas. The trees were going into bloom and leaf: carrots, lettuce, turnips and other kitchen vegetables were fresh for pulling. Before each home, there were roses planted which bloomed very beautifully. Other trees, such as oleander, orange and lemon, were in bloom and could be smelled everywhere.

However, we who had intended to settle in Galveston, did not like conditions here. There were very many mosquitoes and the children were getting sores like smallpox and became sick.

12 March 1850: We left on a steamboat from Galveston for the Brazos River and changed to another steamboat at Quintana at the mouth of the Brazos. We traveled upstream on the Brazos. This was a very exciting trip as there were large trees overhanging the banks. Plantations were located at intervals where we saw negroes working with cotton and sugar cane, all of which grew profusely. There is a large concentration of these unlucky negroes - that is, "slaves" - in Galveston, perhaps as many as 1000 head.

One young strong and healthy slave costs 800 - 1000 dollars per head, a woman slave 500 - 800 dollars, boy from eight to ten years, 100 - 200 dollars; because everybody who is able wishes to buy a slave for work. But so you, even though you are Christians, feel that keeping a human in bondage is not proper, I wish to tell you that these negroes live in a better way than the poor people in Cechy and Moravia. They receive coffee twice a day, meat and bread three times daily, with good milk, as much as they wish, because each plantation has more than 1000 head of livestock. They are occupied with working in the fields, grazing the livestock, and cleaning and butchering same. I saw those slaves playing with the "dollar" same as your boys play with a button.

16 March 1850: Saturday afternoon we arrived at San Felipe; a prominent town destroyed so thoroughly during the war with Mexico that only about fifteen homes remain. Here we stayed with a German merchant who hosted us until the 19th of March. On 17 March, we visited the American rural countryside for the first time and saw pretty tall grass. Cattle freely grazed on it and the children picked the beautiful flowers, some of which in your country are grown in clay flower pots! I and my daughter Julia and the maid Justina, sat down on the grass and sang 'Ja ve vaem mem cineni jen k bohu mam sve zreni' (I in all my deeds have only respect for God), and we thought of you that just now you are returning from the afternoon church services. Here it is 9:45 before noon, and at your place it would be 3:30 in the afternoon since the sun is six and a quarter hours later here.

Tuesday on the day of St. Josef, we loaded our baggage on a wagon and two oxen carried it to our intended place of living, where we happily arrived that same day before night. Here we stayed with a Merchant and farmer named Boulton (Karl Bolton), son of a pastor from Hamburg for whom we had two letters from Europe. We found our stay friendly. Here in his garden, we planted 21 trees which we brought from Europe; also some seed was sown and we planted several rows of potatoes. The surroundings are very beautiful, the soil is black mixed with sand and three fruitful layers deep.

Not far from Mr. Boulton lives a buyer, also from Europe who lives an ugly life. He cheats and wrongly treats his fellow citizens and from this he hopes to become rich.

Tuesday after Palm Sunday, a terrible storm came up and lightning hit the house of the buyer. He had many hundreds of dollars of goods on display and it all burned. No one came to put the fire out because he has had too many quarrels and suits and there were no volunteers. There was no loss to the community and he came to the end of his name. He then moved to Galveston so that he would not have to return to working in the field.

At that same time, the evangelical group met in the community center near Cat Springs, about a mile by the road from Mr. Boulton where it is planned to build a school building. On Saturday before Palm Sunday, I took off for this center so that I could arrange and discuss various things; however it was not possible to do this because it had already been arranged that I was to hold church services at Mr. Boultons on Good Friday. An Evangelical missionary from South Carolina came to this gathering. He was young, healthy and a good speaker, and had already gathered people together to whom he preached. Arrangements were made with him that Easter services would be celebrated at Cat Springs and the Lord's Supper held: and we both left in agreement. On that day (Easter) a larger crowd of people from all sides then gathered, which I had expected, and

# Letters That Sparked German and Czech Emmigration    55

the large room at Mr. Amsler could not contain all of us - the greater number had to stand by the windows and the doors.

At the conclusion of this service, I was voted unanimously to serve as their spiritual pastor and a yearly salary of one hundred dollars was assured me - each voted on this of their own free will and more than one openly agreed to give eight dollars per year. I accepted this assignment and in order to be better able to serve my listeners, I bought myself a small house near Cat Springs, which has one setting room, two closets and a small sleeping room. There is a small three-quarter acre garden near the house and a fifteen acre field which is not plowed.

On the 5th of April, our neighbors came for us with two wagons and we somehow managed to get settled. Today in the afternoon, April 7, 1850, it is planned that we will hold another church service under the same shelter on 17 April unless the listeners decide otherwise. We now have the most beautiful weather and winds; the afternoons are warm but the nights are cool and fine when the fireflies come out and swarm about. The redbirds, here called "Cardinals", sing in the woods and the trees around the house, their song being similar to the nightingale in Europe.

The land here west of San Felipe and five miles from the Brazos River, is not sultry and humid since the winds blow steadily, and there is no fever which exists in some lowlands. There is none of the prevalent human ailments, mainly of the chest, and whoever would come here with a lung ailment will get well quickly. I know two neighbors who, as they told me, with their damaged lungs would already have been laid long ago in their cold bed, whereas here they got completely well. In the lowlands (bottomland) we have very productive lands, so rich that they never need to be fertilized; however, it is unhealthy to live there and for this reason, the colony and settlements is found on the highlands where there is healthy weather. The bottom land fields of the rich planters and settlers is worked by negroes, but the highlands grow Turkish wheat eight to ten feet high. Rye and wheat are not yet planted here as first, there is no mill to grind the grain, and second, it has not been proven to be successfully grown and harvested. Corn, however, grows well in the small valleys and is more productive. So the settlers bake bread made from corn. The corn is ground daily on small hand mills similar to those one has for coffee. The larger corn grain particles are fed to the chickens which everybody here has large flocks of, sometimes in two coops. The small corn flour is prepared with milk and eggs and baked on an iron plate above the coals, although it is still not as good as bread from buckwheat baked in an oven.

Others in the neighboring settlements are able to get enough wheat flour but again there is no bakery or yeast shop, not even a beer brewery. According to a late word, the rumor is out that members of the settlement are planning an Evangelical Church and mill!

Each family has a fenced field here but the remaining land is open and basically used for grazing cattle and horses, however many a person wants; there are hogs beyond count because if you ask someone how many he has, he cannot tell you. "Now I would like to tell you something about our neighbors, but first about the closest.

Ondrej Laass from between Berlin and Magdeburg, lived a long time in Prussia where he saved enough that four years ago he was able and emigrated to America through Bremen. He came alone, had nothing except his healthy body, and had to go to work for others. Now he is well off, has two hundred acres of land, fifty head of cattle, eleven horses and so many hogs that he doesn't even know how many; and to add to that, he has five sons old enough to work and he himself is a strong and diligent worker.

Our other neighbor was a boatman, unloading from the ships in Galveston. Four years ago, he bought land here and now has his own livestock and a healthy sum of cash. Laass, however, has 600 dollars and is thinking of buying a negro for his work.

The third is Haljn who has been here six years and counts among the better-off: he has 100 head of cattle and twenty horses.

However, of all the oldest and first settlers, is surely Mr. Amsler, born a Swiss. He came here more than fifteen years ago, but brought nothing but his health and working hands; and now he has a pretty home, hotel and a store, 1500 acres of land besides two other houses, 300 head of cattle and 100 horses.

From this, it is possible to see that an industrious and working man can soon bring into himself some wealth. However, it is to be noted that 'here without work, there are no kolache!' and anyone who is not industrious will soon return to Europe.

I have already brought two cows with calves for ten dollars and soon will be able to buy a horse so that I may be able to ride in our settlement, or perhaps to San Felipe, some five miles. I already have eighteen hens and a neighbor has promised me some hogs. I will work and fence four acres of field for the fall and will plant cotton because it brings the most. I hope, if God gives me good health, to have more in a few years - but the start is always hard.

Beggars and robbers are not found here and people do not close their doors nor do they have concern for their fields. On our journey, we slept some distance from our wagons and nothing happened to us. In short, no one is concerned about stealing what belongs to others. My wife lost her satchel and in it she had some toiletries and some money. But see, in eight days, our neighbor brought it to us and said it was given to him by a stranger who said it belongs in our settlement!

There are not many people in Texas which is a land as large as Germany and Prussia put together. Texas today has 200,000 inhabitants which is the same as Breslau alone. There are only a few women who are able to come to Texas from Europe and hence these are in great demand. Our maid, Justina, already could have gotten married three times to proper and occupied youths, but she has not yet decided on anyone. Besides that, she has to serve at our home for a time in exchange for the boat fare we paid for her. That will not last long and she will soon leave us and go to her own home and household on a beautiful saddled horse, and if she is fortunate, her groom will bring her the beautiful saddled horse as a gift.

There is here an assortment of various trees such as oaks, maple, nut and so forth. There are forests five miles to the north with cedars and cypresses from which we are able to get boards (lumber). The trees in the forests grow wild, large and tall — from the ground up to the heavens.

You will be able to visualize how it actually all looks from all this I have said, as I have told you the whole clear truth. Whoever wishes to say goodbye to Europe should emigrate through Bremen to America because the ocean voyage from there is better arranged and cheaper than from Hamburg.

I wish to add that here we have many grouse (prairie chickens) and deer. Now, they are shooting turkeys and deer and Mr. Boltin killed a grouse which I saw with my own eyes that weighed twenty pounds. The quail and cranes here are smaller than in Europe but they swarm so no one hardly notices, though they don't stand to be shot. I have not yet had time to go on a hunt. Bees are kept at houses and can be found everywhere in the hollow trees; they swarm from spring to fall - but go into their hives or holes because with the snow and frost, they cannot live. The bees are "robbed" twice, in May and September.

I will repeat once again that emigrants should start on their journey in the fall because in the summer it is dangerous and unhealthy. The best is to organize in groups with families.

You'all be good - God be with you!

..................... (unsigned)

This is a translation of the Bergmann letter dated April 11, 1850 that was published in the *Moravsky Noviny* newspaper later that year. A copy was sent to Albert Blaha by Wolfgang Berndt, a descendent of Mrs. Bergmann who has written articles on Bergmann in Czechoslovakia. The letter was translated by Texas Czech historians Albert Blaha and John Kroulik in 1984.

Ernst Bergmann's wife Marie kept a diary beginning in Silesia in 1848 and continuing until 1871, the year they moved from Cat Spring. Her description of landing at Galveston and moving to Cat Spring indicates that their first stop was in Millheim at the home of Karl Bolton, where Rev. Bergmann preached his first sermon in a tent. They soon moved to a farm near Cat Spring, on which was a small building that was used as a school and community center. Here Bergmann preached and taught for 21 years. Today the site of this first school/church is known as the Kollatschny (or Cat Spring) Cemetery.

# Excerpt from Marie Bergmann Diary

March 2nd, 1850

We stepped on land. Galveston is a city built on wooden boards and every house has a little garden and beautiful trees. The roses are already in bloom and the market has new potatoes. Oh, how good that tasted! We were all moved to the Stern Hotel and it cost us a half a dollar per person a day. After three days we looked for a little place of our own, so we would be able to cook our own food. And our dear Lord sent us to the most wonderful people. They did not charge us for the room and brought us milk and food. It felt so good to find nice people in a strange place. We left them on the 12th of March. On the steamboat we went up the Brazos for four days, before we reached St. Phillips (San Felipe). We expected a city but only found a few broken-down little houses. So we went on three more days by ox cart (one day according to Rev. Bergmann). Mr. Boulton (Karl Bolton) gave us shelter in his little house which he already shared with many chickens, but he was very friendly and we planted our little tree in wine. On Good Friday, Bergmann put up the tent and had church services. Many came. Mr. Guebner (probably Huebner) asked my Bergmann to hold Easter service in Cat Springs, and to hold Communion. After the service they asked us to stay on as pastor. The pay was $84.00 a year. We went to look for a place to stay. Mr. Flatt wanted to sell his little farm, a few cows and chickens, and we bought it for $100. The house was so bad, the rain and wind came through the walls. But God, it was our own!"

# Adolf Fuchs, February 27, 1846

Translation of an article in the 1847 issues No.13 and 15 of the German weekly *Der Deutsche Auswanderer, Centralblatt der deutschen Auswanderung und Kolonisirung* — Darmstadt, Germany, which reprinted a letter, dated February 27, 1846, written by Pastor Adolf Fuchs in Cat Spring to his relatives in Germany. The letter was translated by Ernest A. Guenther of Austin, Texas, in 1970, whose parenthetical notes introduce the letter, written within weeks of their arrival at Cat Spring.

Fuchs addressed his letter to August Hoffmann von Fallersleben[9], a fellow poet and lyricist whom he had met shortly before leaving for Texas:

---

9  August Heinrich Hoffmann von Fallersleben was a German poet, scholar, librettist, and author of Texas lyrics. He wrote the lyrics to *Lied der Deutschen*, aka. *Deutschlandlied*, a song that became one of the symbols of the March Revolution of 1848, the aftermath of which brought many immigrants to Texas. The song has since been adopted as the national anthem of Germany. He began an association with Texas in 1843 when he came in contact with Gustav Dresel, a German who had returned from spending four years in the Houston area as a merchant and cotton exporter. While working with Dresel on a journal of his experiences in Texas, Hoffmann also befriended Adolf Fuchs just a few weeks before the Fuchs family sailed for Texas in late 1845. For their departure Hoffmann wrote his first poem about the Lone Star emblem, "Der Stern von Texas", now called the Texas German anthem. The two men began work on Dresel's Texas journal, which was published in Germany with the false statement on the title page saying it was written by Texas Germans and published in San Felipe by "Adolph Fuchs & Co.". It has been republished as *Gustav Dresel's Houston Journal*, (Austin: University of Texas Press, 1954).

Hoffmann completed his collection of thirty-one Texas songs, *Texanische Lieder*, in 1846. In order to circumvent censorship regulations, Hoffmann had the title page state that the book was written by German Texans and published in San Felipe, Texas, by "Adolf Fuchs & Co.," whereas it actually came out in Wandsbeck, Germany.

(Dresel, Gustav. *The Handbook of Texas Online,* Texas State Historical Association (TSHA). *Tshaonlineorg*. 2017. Available at: https://tshaonline.org/handbook/online/articles/fdr02. Accessed September 7, 2017.; Deutschlandlied. *Enwikipediaorg*. 2017. Available at: https://en.wikipedia.org/wiki/Deutschlandlied. Accessed September 7, 2017..)

## Letters From Texas

(The poet Hoffmann von Fallersleben, by whose courtesy we are permitted to reprint the following letter, remarks about its author: Adolph Fuchs was a protestant clergyman at Koelzow in the Rostock area. For many years he filled the position of pastor to the satisfaction of his small congregation. His income was very limited, so that in the course of time he had to use up his own and his wife's means. Since he could not agree with the theological views of the church authorities, which were old-orthodox and bigoted, he could never expect any pecuniary improvement in his position. Therefore, he decided to emigrate and give his large family a better future and to find for himself a vocation more in agreement with his convictions. In the autumn of 1845 he said farewell to his congregation (his farewell sermon has been printed), boarded a sailing ship in Bremen and, around Christmas time of the same year, he and his loved ones landed safely in Galveston. He is a man of sterling character, full of determination, energy and endurance, and yet a charming personality, endowed by nature with these most precious talents: He teaches, preaches, writes, speaks several languages, does wood-turning and carpentry, knows about agriculture and gardening, plays the violin, piano and guitar, and is outstanding as a singer. The information in his letter is of great interest to his friends, his relatives, and others.)

Fallersleben, Wild-Cat-Spring, Austin County, Texas

February 27, 1846

To all my loved ones in Europe, brothers, sisters, uncles, aunts, nephews, nieces and others! I am completely at ease and in excellent spirits as I sit on a home-made bench in our small farm house, surrounded by my wife and children who are tending the stove, while I am thinking of you. For the present—perhaps for good — we have left the German colony (i.e. The Adelsverein, or Association for the Protection of German Immigrants in Texas) which had made more promises than it could keep, and have traveled to this location on our own, which is a two-day journey (by horse) northwest of Houston. We are at the "spring of the Wild cats" in the immediate neighborhood of Albrecht von Roeder, Wilhelm von Roeder, the elder von Roeders, Robert and Louis Kleberg, Engelking (all are former lawyers), Hollien, Amseler (a Swiss), Amthor and others. We have bought for only $ 200.- a ready farm of a few hundred acres[10]. These people have treated us with the utmost friendliness and they are continuously interested in getting us well settled, so that, in spite of limited funds, we do not worry about the future. Twelve acres are enclosed with a good fence, and additional acres can easily be cleared for cultivation. The houses (three log-houses) are good but rather small for us. However, our neighbors are going to build us this summer a larger house as prepayment for my services of teaching their children in addition to my own during the coming winter. A school house also will be built, not only for the instruction of children, but also as a community center. On the days when community parties are being held, every family of the settlement brings some food and drinks, and the activities include good conversation, bowling, target shooting, playing chess, and above all singing and dancing, etc. Yes, the house is also intended for more serious gatherings, similar to your churches, but only similar. Heinrich Fuchs will possibly assist in teaching, also our oldest children. This summer we will probably have no classes, but in future summers possibly twice a week a few hours, so that the children will not forget what they learned during the winter.

Our neighbors plowed part of our land three weeks ago, and I have already planted 56 peach and plum trees; besides onions and peas I have planted many seeds, mainly peach stones which bear fruit in the third year; I prepared tobacco beds with seeds from Havana. The Texas-grown tobacco is excellent, and I

---

10  On February 9, 18 days before this letter.

am smoking now a cigar made from local tobacco leaves. During autumn we all will make cigars. We also planted German potatoes, next will be sweet potatoes and then corn. For the present we do not want to plant any cotton.

As far as animals are concerned, we own at this time one cow and have two more "on loan", to which will be added in the near future four to six more on a loan basis. With this loan arrangement we are actually doing our neighbors a favor, since they are unable to milk all their cows themselves. We also have 13 laying hens which were given to us besides a cat and a dog. In about 4 weeks we have consumed almost one pig, ¼ ox, two deer and a few bushels of corn from which we make bread and cooked cereal. Tomorrow I will try to do some plowing with two oxen, and later with a strong horse which we will buy in exchange for a surplus piece of equipment since our financial reserves are practically exhausted. We were foolish to take so many items with us, but this is excusable as the Association (Adelsverein) was going to take care of transportation, for which it now lacks the necessary funds. I feel sorry for the very poor immigrants who are stranded at the coast and who just have to wait. You who intend to follow us listen to our urgent advice: Sell everything except your clothing and shoes and bring only money along. Sell everything, including those items which you believe to be able to put to excellent use over here, as for German rifles, the latter are not usable in this country where only American rifles are practical. At most, you should take along some seeds packed in dry sand and some cooking utensils, such as copper kettles, coffee pots etc. We have made a close calculation which shows that a family such as yours in Goldberg needs not more than 1100 Reichthaler in order to establish a home here on our land and to buy the necessary stock and equipment. We are unable to work all our land anyway and besides, we expect for our children the considerable legacy of a soldier land grant west of here. There is no doubt that we will get the land, less one third—as is customary here—in payment for the services of a lawyer in Houston who is handling the legal formalities. The soil over here can be considered an average of the type found in Texas, and yet the corn grows 12 to 15 feet high and even higher; melons get very large, and all garden produce thrives much better than in Germany. However, the main wealth over here is live stock, especially cattle which only requires some money when you buy it, and nothing more for its maintenance. Our main endeavor, therefore, will be the acquisition of a good stock of cattle in exchange for some of our surplus articles, as for fine table linen and other luxury items, an expensive double-barrel shotgun (a combination shotgun and rifle), etc. I still have one rifle and two shotguns. A cow and calf cost 310.- while horses are priced the same as in Europe. To get water at our farm is somewhat inconvenient about 500 to 600 paces from the house, however, we have already a sled with a barrel and we are negotiating for a horse. Later we can dig a well, which is easy to do as one lines the hole with oak planks. This is particularly easy at a spot between our farm and what I like to think of as your farm my dear Goldbergers, because there you will find at a shallow depth of often not more than ½ foot, firm loam covered with black fertile sand.

The tree coverage in Texas, and especially here at Cat Spring is rather moderate. The grass, however, grows very luxuriantly here at the border of the prairie and extending toward the Brazos river. Therefore this settlement is ideally suited for stock raising, better than the wooded areas on the Mills and Cummins creeks. Keeping of bees is very profitable over here. We will start with one or several bee-hives , since it is customary for the people to give them away, as well as piglets — in the same manner that the people of Germany give away their kittens.

For the present this is enough about animals. Now, the people here are really outstanding, and our association with such people within a walking distance, could never be duplicated in Germany. This is no exaggeration. There is little, very little, comfort of the type espoused by the English people. Our houses are cabins, our clothes are poor, our beds are hard, our hands often dirty — but our hearts are free and gay! Incidentally, we have decided to do more for our comfort than is customary by the local German settlers and particularly by those who are former German scholars. They may be wiser in this respect, but whether they are happier is still a question. I think, however, there is a middle road.

My dear Moserin, for people like you who can take with them some loyal white workers, the chances of good earnings are excellent. As soon as one is well settled here, the need for workers for the cultivation of the fields is of primary importance. Live stock does not require any work. It is a joy to see our cows and calves coming to the pen every evening. So far, Lulu does the milking of the cows, but she will shortly have Ulla as an assistant, and then it is Ottilie's turn. Our settlement and particularly our farm have the great advantage of being located directly on the main road of Texas, where people come to our door and buy farm produce for cash. We live on the road from Houston to the capital city of Austin.

We advise anyone who wants to follow us, to travel on his own from Hamburg to Galveston, without the aid of the noblemen's association (Adelsverein). From there take a steamship (which departs almost daily) to Houston and buy horses and wagon. (Unless you have brought wheels and steel axles with you, which can be attached in Houston to a wooden frame in order to produce a broad-gauge local wagon—the wagons cost here four or five times as much as in Germany). When the roads are in good condition, it takes from Houston to Cat Spring three or at most four days. Then you can establish yourselves on our farm or buy some land and a house. However, in the winter, that is from Christmas until now and even later, the roads are terrible. We have not had any freezing temperatures to speak of, there was almost no ice, but the north wind is cold. In Houston you should buy flour and meat (beef is 2 cents and pork 4 cents a pound, which is the equivalent of 1 and 2 shillings). It is also recommended to bring from Europe a good tent for camping, its canvas can be used later for other purposes. If there is enough room, you can also sleep under the wagon's tarpaulin, and ship at least some of your belongings by freight. This is the way we did it. There are also inns along the way. I promised a special letter to you my dear Wilhelm Wien, but I like to be excused for not carrying out my promise. There is nothing special I can write to you, but I believe that you would enjoy the way of life over here. If you like a somewhat wild and restless life you can emulate Heinrich Fuchs and Ludwig Franke, who are taking a trip through Texas and are trying to join the Texas Rangers, guarding the borders against Mexicans and Indians, at a monthly salary of $ 20.- plus free food and lodging. They want to leave, as I and Conrad are able to take care of our small farm adequately, and the big daughters together with their mother can take care of the household chores. I believe, however, that they will return before long, at least after half a year. In the Rangers you have to enlist for a minimum of 6 months and you have to bring along a good horse and a good rifle..... [11]

The following information was obtained from the 1850 US Census: Benjamin Fuchs (son of Adolf Fuchs) is listed as being two years old and born in Texas. This indicates that his sister Ottilie stated incorrectly that he was born in Koelzow Germany. The U.S. Census further reveals that Adolf Fuchs had 7 acres improved land and 92 acres unimproved land, four horses, 13 milch cows, 12 other cattle, and 16 pigs. His harvest for the previous year was 80 bushels corn, 200 lbs. tobacco, 90 bushels Irish potatoes, 40 bushels sweet potatoes, 400 lbs. Butter and one ton of hay.

Adolph Fuchs immediately began seeking sources of financing to build a new school. In 1849 he sent the following petition to the state legislature:

"To the Hon Senate & House of Representatives of the State of Texas. "Memorandum "Thirty German families at Cat Springs and in the neighborhood, feeling the necessity of having an

---

11 The concluding chapter of Adolf Fuchs' letter is missing in the UT files.

English school for their numerous children, are building a convenient schoolhouse, and the underscribed is appointed their first teacher.

"But, though these families are convinced that a School is an indispensable requisite to them, as well as that English schools are undeniably the best way to americanize the german population of Texas and to make good citizens of them and that good schools are undoubtedly the bulwark of the Republic - still most of the said families are poor and accordingly their means insufficient to maintain a good school. On the contrary, their exertions will probably be of little success, if not quite lost, "Unless the government of the State of Texas will sustain them! "They hope, therefore, the government will not refuse their request, and the Senator of their County, General Portis, will be their intervener.

"Cat Springs Adolphus Fuchs

"Oct. the 29th, 1849 in the name and commission of 30 german families of Cat Springs and the neighborhood."

There is no record of any state aid deriving from this request.

# Millheim

Millheim is a half-Americanized German word meaning the home of a mill. It was never a town in the usual sense, but rather a rural community consisting of several family farms with their dwelling houses strung along a couple of miles of bluff bordering the south bank of Mill Creek in Austin County, Texas, between San Felipe and Cat Spring. There was no central business district, although a mercantile store, a grist mill, a medical clinic/pharmacy and a school were operated by residents out of their homes. The most enduring feature remaining today is the Millheim Harmonie Verein hall, established by local residents in 1872 to carry on the community's German traditions and provide a place for entertainment and social activities.

Permanent settlement in the area began in the late 1830s and early 1840s by Americans who arrived and purchased tracts in the Cumings Mill Tract and the Miles Allen grant. German settlement in the Millheim began in 1840 when Louis and Louise von Roeder Kleberg built a home on Clear Creek. In 1842 Ferdinand Friedrich Engelking moved onto a labor (177 acres) in the Miles Allen grant, located on Louis Kleberg's western boundary. He bought it in 1845 from Louis Kleberg. Engelking had arrived in 1840, soon marrying Caroline von Roeder. Others began arriving the mid—late 1840s, predominately Germans joining other countrymen who had arrived in Texas more than a decade earlier. Many of the Millheim pioneers were known as Forty-Eighters, Germans who had participated in or supported the revolutions of 1848 that swept Europe. They had attempted to overthrow the petty monarchy system that existed in Germany at that time, failed, and were forced to leave. Most were highly educated, leading to their becoming known in Texas as Lateiners, as most read and spoke Latin. In Texas, they had no choice but to farm to survive.

Five Lateiner communities were established in Texas. Two were in Austin County — Millheim and Latium. The others were Bettina (near Kingsland, Llano County), Sisterdale and Tusculum (later changed to Boerne) in Kendall County. Bettina soon folded; Boerne and Sisterdale remain as towns today. Millheim and Latium survived as extended rural communities of German- and Czech-American residents.

Sigismund Engelking told how Millheim received its name: "In the fifties a meeting was held in my father's first store, which he conducted in partnership with Nolte, for the purpose of giving our settlement a name. Naturally I was a spectator, but I can't recall all the details. I do remember, however, that toward evening the meeting became very jolly. Barrels of tar were lighted and bets for wine and other drinks were made as to who could jump through the flames. A certain Quensel, also known as the Ranger, didn't jump high enough and fell into a burning barrel, searing his legs badly before the others could pull him out. Dr. Nagel smeared oil on his burns and the drinking and merriment, as well as the wrestling and racing went right on into the night. Dr. Nagel was the best jumper, and I always envied him for his achievements in this art. Such were the 'Schwabenstreichle', Swabian feats, in which the old Texans delighted. During this hilarious meeting the name Muehlheim was chosen at the suggestion of Wilhelm Schneider, who came from the Rhine - Palatinate, but it wasn't long before the Anglo- Americans had botched it up into Millheim."[12]

The first school in Millheim was located on the farm of Ferdinand Engelking. It opened in 1850 with two pupils, Sigismund

---

12  Trenckmann W. *Experiences And Observations*. Austin, Texas: The Family; 2015.
    The place name Millheim is specifically mentioned in *Engelking letters* dated 1853.

Engelking and Anna Hagemann. Gustav Ernst Maetze was the teacher and soon gained a favorable reputation, attracting more students from local as well as more remote communities. A larger school was built mid-way between the Engelking and Kloss homes; it was destroyed by an arsonist during the Civil War. After the war, Maetze reopened the school in the parlor of his house in Millheim. Soon thereafter a new schoolhouse was built in 1867, where Maetze, his wife and daughter, Sigismund Engelking, Fred Kloss and others taught.

Millheim resident Adalbert Regenbrecht wrote: "E.G. Maetze escaped to Texas. He went to New Ulm and worked for a farmer. Hunting a horse in the Bernard Prairie he met F. Engelking, who invited him to become a tutor of his children. Maetze accepted the proposal and a short while afterwards he established the first school in Millheim with six pupils at forty dollars per pupil in the first year. ... The number of pupils grew from year to year, not only from the neighborhood but also from distant places. He taught school at Millheim more than twenty-five years." The Millheim school closed in 1949.

Millheim and its nearby neighboring communities Clarksville, Cleveland, Peters and Hacienda were described by Sigismund Engelking and printed by William Trenckmann in the 1899 "A History of Austin County" supplement to his newspaper, the *Bellville Wochenblatt*:

"Today this settlement includes five school communities and all of them vote at the Millheim Box at the Harmonie Halle in old Millheim. The communities are Millheim, Clarksville, Peters, Cleveland and Hacienda; altogether they have about 200 votes and about 275 children of school age.

"The boundaries of Millheim are Mill Creek to the north, from its mouth into the Brazos about ten miles up the creek, then to the west eight miles to the Bernard and ten miles southward along this stream; and finally eastward from there about fifteen miles back to the starting point. The western boundary extends to within two miles of Cat Spring and the eastern boundary just as near to Sealy. ...

"I cannot state with historical accuracy just how far back the beginnings of Millheim go, since no one could ever tell me anything definite about it...neither old Mr. E. Swearingen, who came in 1836 from Corpus Christi to Mill Creek Settlement, as this region was then called, nor my dear old Aunt Louise Kleberg. In about the year 1840 she and her husband built a house in the black jack grove near the Langhammer burial ground and put a three-acre tract under cultivation.

"Only this much is certain: the first settlers were squatters who lived somewhat to the north of the Bolten place. This was in the Twenties. One of them, a so-called Tyler, planted a special kind of half-wild plum tree there, which continued to grow and bear fruit in various thickets for twenty years after his death, fruit which was picked every year by my parents, who came in 1842 to the place where my dear mother still lives. There was also a white, or very light-colored, wine made of mustang grapes, which grow wild in this area and may have been introduced into the Mill Creek Paradise by the same gardener.

"It is too bad that the good man did not remain there. We might have learned much about fruit growing from him. But the squatters of that time were in general wild, reckless fellows, who often came into conflict with their neighbors or with the law and consequently were always seeking new hunting grounds, where they could live undisturbed in a sweet state of idleness.

This must have been Tyler's way, too, for in 1842 not a trace of a house could be seen, nor of his clearing on Clear Creek on exactly the same place where our friend Heinrich Schroeder later battled with the floods of this creek, which is subject to such rapid rises. By 1842 a dense forest of young trees had shot up again on the deserted field.

"In Tyler's time, yes, and even when I was a boy, Clear Creek was an entirely different stream than today. There was one deep water hole after another, so deep that we boys had to learn to swim in these pools. And overhead a dense roof of wild peach trees shut out every ray of the sun. That is all past and gone now. The creek has flattened out and sanded up. In those days it was never dry. None of the lovely evergreen trees are left, and probably not one can be found in the entire Clear Creek Valley.

"The squatters left with their Kentucky rifles on their shoulders, and permanent settlers, who bought the land on which to build their homes, replaced them. They came in approximately the following order: E. Swearingen, V. Swearingen, Louis Kleberg, Sapp, who had a hotel on the road from San Felipe to upper Texas where Adolph Necker's road now crosses the railroad tracks. Then came F. Engelking, Carl Wenmohs, Marcus and Fritz Amsler, H. Vornkahl, H. Bolten, Ernst Kleberg, Louis Constant (he wanted to make Mill Creek navigable), W. Mersman, A. Hagemann (inventor of tomato cider), F. Langhammer, Emil Kloss, Alex Kloss, J. A. Wilm (he built the first gin in Millheim), Robert Kloss (he built the first sorghum press), J. H. Krancher (the first constable), Rudolph Goebel, Wilhelm Schneider, Carl Schneider, August and Otto Goebel, F. Buntzel, Theodor Brosig, B. Siegert, E. G. Maetze (founder of the old Millheim school), A. F. Trenckmann (father of the first Agricultural Society in Texas), F. Heinieke, Dr. Nagel, A. Regenbrecht, and A. Kluewer, all from Germany. The majority came with their families, and the rest married here.

"Most of these men are dead and buried; only a half dozen of the old guard, who have not yet surrendered, are still with us.

"Clarksville was founded by old man Clark, Manor, and Allen, the gunsmith. This Allen alone supplied arms for the infantry of the Austin County contingent of the Army of Texas Volunteers, which went to San Antonio in 1842 to defend it from the Mexicans. Allen marched from Clarksville to San Antonio on foot because he had no horse and didn't want to stay behind; but since the Mexicans didn't arrive, Allen marched back home on foot again without catching sight of a single enemy. F. Hillboldt, Gottlieb, Sam and Claus Hillboldt were also among the first settlers of Clarksville.

"Cleveland was first settled by Salomo and Eckhardt above the Buzzard Roost on the San Bernard.

"Peters, or Millheim Station, was really founded by Emil Deharpe, who lived on Dead Man's Creek and earned his livelihood making shingles. Later came Sens, Sr. and Jr., Loehr, Buller, Hintz, Grabow, etc. Since the coming of the Santa Fe, this area has built up much faster; and, like Old Millheim, it has a store, a postoffice, its own gin, a blacksmith shop and even a doctor.

"About twenty-five years ago Fritz and Carl Schroeder were the first to settle in Hacienda. Up to that time it was considered unhealthy for human beings to live in this area. But it doesn't seem to be too bad, for besides the Schroeders, about 30 other families live there, and every year new ones arrive.

"In regard to the soil itself and its possibilities, we should add that the whole northern stretch along Mill Creek is heavy black land of great productivity, which is flooded now and then, and, like the Nile Valley, is in reality always renewed; thus inexhaustible fertility remains because of the floods. Farther south the soil is mixed and still farther south, pure sand. But the prosperous condition of the farmers on the prairies proves that is is not too bad even there."

# Pioneer Settlers in the Cat Spring/ Millheim Corridor

Many of these individuals were much better educated than most immigrants of the time. Among them were professors, lawyers, doctors, goldsmiths and merchants. Here in Texas they were virtually all forced into farming as the mainstay of their livelihood, although some continued to practice their trades as an adjunct to farming. They and their children proved to be exceptional achievers, remarkable in number of very successful individuals for such a small of population segment. Following is a listing of many of these early settlers, with a brief historical summary of each. Information for these biographies consists of summaries from the Cat Spring Story for many individuals, plus added material from research by the authors.

### *AMSLER*

Carl Conrad Amsler was one of the original Cat Spring settlers, arriving in 1834 from Canton Aargau, Switzerland. He participated in the Siege of Bexar in 1835, and the enlisted for the Matamoros Expedition but fell ill, thereupon being given an honorable discharge[13]. After the revolution he established a tavern and a stage coach stand in Cat Spring. He also operated a farm with grist mill and gin. He made several trips to Switzerland bring back able bodied families who worked for him to repay the costs of their passage.[14]

---

13  *The Sons Of The Republic Of Texas.* Paducah, Ky.: Turner Pub. Co.; 2001.
14  Amsler's 1835/6 experiences are given in the book titled *Johan Spiess: Survivor of the*

Marcus Amsler came from Switzerland in 1837 and settled in Millheim.

## AMTHOR

Henry Amthor came from Germany to Texas in 1837 and settled near Cat Spring where he engaged in farming and ranching. He was amongst the families trying to establish Hermann's University which did not come to fruition. His wife would accompany Adoph Fuchs on the piano[15] because the Fuchs family stayed in their house until they could establish themselves[16].

## BERGMANN

Rev. Joseph Arnost Bergman arrived at Cat Spring from Strausny, Silesia, in 1850. An ordained Lutheran minister, he preached, farmed and taught school in a small log building. A lengthy letter he wrote soon after he arrived extolled the freedoms, resources and opportunities of his new home. The letter was widely circulated in Bohemnia and Moravia, and served as the springboard for the large migration of Czechs to Texas that began in 1852.[17]

## BOLTEN

Karl Bolten arrived in Millheim in 1842, where he purchased a farm from a man named Tyler, who had arrived around 1835.

## BOSTICK

The Levi Bostick family moved from Alabama to Texas in 1829, locating initially on Mill Creek near Cat Spring. They also had a land grant on the county line west of Cat Spring, and blazed a

---

*Matamoros Expedition, Carriage Driver for the Angel of Goliad and Father of Two Civil War Soldiers* by James Woodrick, available on amazon.com)

15  Goyne M. *Lone Star And Double Eagle: Civil War Letters Of A German-Texas Family*. Texas Christian University / English; 1982.

16  Goeth O, Guenther I. *Memoirs Of A Texas Pioneer Grandmother*. Burnet, Tex.: Eakin Pr.; 1982.

17  Woodrick J. *The First Czech Texans: Snippets Of Texas History Series (Volume 3)*. amazon.com; 2017.

road between these two locations that became known as the Bostick trace. Most of the family moved to near Columbus in 1831; James H. Bostick remained.

## BROSIG

Theodore Brosig's parents settled in Cat Spring in 1850.

## BUCHTIEN

Christian Christopher Herman Buchtien and his family settled near Cat Spring in 1851.

## CLARKE

Edwin N. Clarke was one of the original settlers of area that would become Cat Spring, arriving around 1830. His daughter Sarah married Elemenech Swearingen, the other pioneer settler in this area. He was postmaster in Cat Spring from 1861-1866[18].

## CONSTANT

Louis Constant was an early Millheim settler, an actor and a marginal farmer. Constant was viewed as a visionary and promoted making Constant Creek (named after him) navigable through Mill Creek and the Brazos to the Gulf of Mexico, thus creating Millheim as a port city. He eventually had his fill of Texas and returned to Germany when he lost title to his land as a result of a lawsuit decision in 1868.

## DITTERT

Christian Leopold Dittert and family arrived in Cat Spring in 1848, receiving a land grant in which the modern town of Cat Spring is situated.

---

[18] Wheat, J. *Postmasters and Post Offices of Texas, 1846-1930* at 13. Austin County, Texas. Available at: http://www.rootsweb.ancestry.com/~txpost/austin.html. Accessed September 7, 2017.

## ENGELKING

Friedrich Ferdinand Engelking first set foot in Texas on January 1, 1840. He proceeded to Cat Spring where he lived for a while with Kleberg and bought land in Millheim in 1845.

He was born the son of the Mayor of Schlüsselburg near Minden in Prussia. Today, Schlüsselburg is a tiny village but at that time it was an important administrative location. After Friedrich Ferdinand's father died, he was entitled to his share of the inheritance which his mother was holding on his behalf. This provided him with the funding to make the hazardous journey to Texas. He had studied at Heidelberg University and become a lawyer but he could not face the thought of doing legal work in the suffocating atmosphere of Prussia at the time. He was also inspired by democratic ideals and a strong sense of adventure. Accordingly, without telling any of his relatives, he set sail for New Orleans on September 11 1839 on the Bremer sailing ship "Julia" with the intention of becoming a farmer. He sent a letter just before leaving to his sister and brother-in-law informing them of his decision. Finding no suitable prospects in New Orleans, he decided to move on to Texas having heard from the von Roeder's and Kleberg with whom he already enjoyed friendship[19]. He ended up marrying the youngest child of the von Roeders, Ottilie Elisabeth Caroline Louise von Roeder in 1842 with whom he had 11 children. The family still holds together and holds regular family reunions in the Millheim Har-

*Friedrich Ferdinand Engelking with Wife Caroline née von Roeder*

---

19 This information has been extracted from the pioneer's own words which can be found in *The Engelking Letters* mentioned elsewhere in this book.

monie Verein Hall to this day on land which he and Heinrich Vornkahl donated.

Apart from being active in the Cat Spring Agricultural Society and running his farm, he was also Justice of the Peace for a while. A believer, as all Germans, in the value of education, he founded the high school ("gymnasium") in Millheim after a fortuitous meeting with Ernst Gustav Maetze in the prairie.

The historic Engelking cemetery is located near the site of the once Engelking house which was destroyed by fire.

As an interesting aside, Ferdinand Engelking owned a slave, referred to as Uncle Wash, who became like a member of the family and remained so until his death. He appears to have been not only a servant in the household, but also a protector of the young Engelking children, the latter which cost him his life. The family obtained their water from the creek of springs which ran near their home. One day Ferdinand's wife Lina Engelking sent the boys to the spring at the edge of the woods to fetch a supply of water. As they neared the site, several Indians sprang after them and cut off their escape back to the house. Wash had just stepped out of his little house and witnessed what was happening. He ran toward the main house waving his arms and shouting. The noise he created drew the Indians' attention to him and they began chasing him instead of the boys. This allowed Lina to load her old shotgun with buckshot and take aim. She fired several times while the Indians chased Wash back to his house and the children rushed to safety. The sound of the shots caused the Indians to duck back into the woods, thus allowing Wash to escape back to the safety of his house.

All was silence from Wash's quarters for a long time. Lina, who was expecting him to help her in the main house, went to investigate. She found Wash dead on the floor of his cabin. Apparently, the fright and excitement had been too much for his old heart. A hero for saving the children, Wash was given a burial place in the corner of the Engelking family cemetery on the hillside overlooking Millheim. Several of the deceased Engelking children slept there, so he was laid to rest among them[20].

## FUCHS

Carl Adolf Friedrich Fuchs was from Mecklenburg, in northern Germany. As a youth he enjoyed outdoor activities and he learned to play the violin. He entered university at the age of eighteen and studied theology and philosophy at the Universities of Halle, Berlin, Rostock, and Jena. He married Luise Rumker in 1829, and for the next six years taught school in Waren. He became pastor at the Lutheran church in Kolzow in 1835, and preached there for ten years. He became interested in emigration to North America, and in 1836 he published a poem called "The New Fatherland." During this time he also wrote a novel dealing with a young theological student-minister who eventually became very critical of the conditions of the Evangelical Church in Germany in the 1830s and decided to emigrate to North America. The novel *Robert* was published in Rostock in 1842.

*Carl Adolf Friedrich Fuchs*

In 1844 he obtained a certificate for a quarter-league of land (1,107 acres) on the Colorado river in Texas that had initially been awarded to a participant in the Texas Revolution, and later sold. Fuchs became disenchanted with the strict orthodoxy then being practiced by church authorities, and had begun receiving criticism for the views he expressed in his novel. He applied to emigrate to Texas under the auspices of the Adelsverein, and finally was given room on a ship that left in 1845. Fuchs gave up his ministry when he left Germany. When they arrived in

---

20   This story is taken from: von Roeder F. *These Are The Generations*. [Texas]: [F. von Roeder]; 2014.

Galveston they learned of a fever epidemic in Indianola, their intended destination, so they debarked at Galveston and made their way to Cat Spring. They bought a farm which provided most of their sustenance; Fuchs also taught school in a new schoolhouse/community center, and taught music at the Institute for Young Ladies at Independence, the forerunner of Baylor University. After eight years, they finally obtained title to their land on the Colorado, and moved to near Marble Falls where they lived the remainder of their lives.

While the family was living in Cat Spring, they established a lasting friendship with the family of Johannes Romberg, who had emigrated from Mecklenburg in 1847. Romberg was also a renowned German poet in Texas. Eventually, two of the Fuchs sons married Romberg daughters.

## *GOEBEL*

Rudolph Goebel emigrated from Dollstadt, Germany in 1849 and bought a farm near Millheim.

## *HAGEMANN*

Albert Hagemann, from Halle Sachsen, Germany, settled in Millheim in 1846. One of the Latieners, he had been a merchant prior to Texas, where he farmed. He is credited with inventing tomato cider. His son William Hagemann became a Deputy Collector of the US Internal Revenue Service in Sherman.

## *HILLBOLDT*

Two related men both named Samuel Hillboldt from Canton Aargau, Switzerland, were recruited to come to Texas by Charles Amsler. They settled between Millheim and Cat Spring in the old Clarksville community in 1848, where they farmed and ranched.

## HIMLEY

Alexander and Clothinda Himley settled in the Berdardo / Cat Spring area in 1848. He had studied agriculture in college before coming to Texas, where he introduced new seeds and trees, and an improved breed of sheep.

## HINTZE

Joachim Hintze was 14 years of age when he settled with his family near Millheim in 1855; they came from Mecklenburg. After participating in the Civil War and becoming a prisoner of war in Mississippi, he returned to become a farmer and noted baumeister, or master carpenter. Three of his signature buildings still stand today - the main pavilion in the Bellville City Park, built originally for the Turnverin Gut Heil society in 1897, the dance hall at Peters (built 1900) and the Cat Spring Agricultural Society hall (built 1903).

## HOLLIEN

In the letter from Engelking, dated February 1841, he mentions Hollien as a potential partner, indicating that the latter was single like Engelking himself. He returned to Germany a couple of years later and returned with a wife. According to *The Cat Spring Story*, Johann (Hans) Hollien and Hulda Ramm were married in Rostock, Mecklenburg, on March 21 1844, a son was born to them in Galveston on December 6, 1845, after which they came by ox-wagon to Cat Spring where they settled among the other German settlers.

## KEUFFEL

Wilhelm Keuffel emigrated from Hamburg in 1852, initially settled near Cat Spring, then moved to Millheim in 1853, he farmed and made cigars commercially. His son William L.E., born in Millheim, became a prominent Hoboken, New Jersey manufacturer of precision instruments in the partnership formed by his second cousin William J.D. Kueffel and Herman

Esser in 1867. Their K&E slide rules were a mainstay for engineering students and practicing engineers in the 1940s, 50s, and 60s.

## *KLEBERG*

*Robert Justus Kleberg*

Robert Justus Kleberg came to Texas in 1834 with his wife Rosalie, her von Roeder parents and other relatives including his brother Louis Kleberg. They settled in Cat Spring near the von Roeders. He participated in the Battle of San Jacinto, was president of the Republic of Texas Land Commissioners in 1838, Chief Justice of Austin County in 1846 before moving to DeWitt County in 1847. His son Robert, Jr. married Alice Gertrudis King, daughter of Richard and Henrietta King, becoming the patriarch of the Kleberg family that owns the massive King Ranch.

## *KLOSS*

Emil Kloss and his wife came to Texas in 1850 from Mecklenberg (Rostock), settling near Millheim. His brothers Robert and Alex soon joined them. Emil returned to Germany. Robert was a jeweler and goldsmith by trade, but farmed by proxy in Texas.

## *KOY*

Franz Koy and Matilda Ratuschny Koy arrived in Texas in 1853 and settled in the Bernardo / Cat Spring area where they farmed and raised cattle. Their descendants included Austin County sheriff George Koy and professional baseball/football players Ernest Koy, Sr. and Jr.

## LAAS

Johann Laas came from Saxony to the Cat Spring / Millheim area in 1844.

## LANGHAMMER

Franz Langhammer was a wine-maker and merchant from Josefstadt, near Prague, in Bohemia. He and his wife Marie Kratky had a large family of some eleven children. Langhammer was "a revolutionary" and came alone to Texas in 1848; his family followed in 1849. They settled on a farm east of Millheim on the road to San Felipe.

## LESHIKAR

Joseph Lidumil Leshikar and family came to Texas from Bohemia in 1853 and settled west of Cat Spring in the New Bremen area. He organized the first group migrations of Czechs to Texas in 1851 and 1853.

## MAETZE

*Gustav Maetze*

Ernst Gustav Maetze[21], teacher and legislator, was born in Silesia and graduated from the University of Breslau with a degree in Protestant theology. He became headmaster of the intermediate school at Bernstadt in Silesia. He participated in the German revolutionary movement of 1848 and in the early 1850s and was forced to emigrate to Texas, where he first taught at

---

21 Ernst Gustav Maetze (1817-1891). According to the *Texas Historical State Archives*, he was married to Marie Langhammer – granddaughter of Franz Langhammer mentioned on page 88. (Miller Family Papers). He taught in the school in Millheim, retiring around 1878 and was elected in 1888 to the Texas Senate.
Available at: https://tshaonline.org/handbook/online/articles/fma11. Accessed September 8, 2017., August 27, 2017).

a private school at Millheim. Shortly afterwards he founded the first public school in Millheim and subsequently taught there for twenty-seven years. In 1888 he was elected to the Texas Senate where he chaired the Committee on Rules and was president pro tem of the Senate when he died in Millheim in 1891. L.E. Daniell[22] writes about his political career:

> The venerable Senator, E.G.Maetze, son of G. F. and A. M. Maetze, of Prussia, was born in Glogau Silesia, a Prussian Province, and educated first in the gymnasium, and then took an academic course in the University of Breslau.
>
> In his youth Senator Maetze was deeply indoctrinated with Democratic principles, and during a service in the German Diet in 1848 and 1849, he manifested such an opposition to a monarchical form of government, and became such a bold and able champion of the largest liberties consistent with a plain and Democratic government, that he was convicted of treason and sentenced to one years imprisonment. He fled his native country and sought refuge on the hospitable shores of Texas. He arrived in Texas, in 1850, and his devotion to his adopted country is even greater than a native, for he knows how galling the oppression of monarchy is upon those who dare to think for themselves.
>
> Having studied, especially Philology, when he arrived in Texas he settled in Austin county and taught school in the same place for twenty-eight years, and has served as school superintendent of Austin county.
>
> In 1861 he was a member of Sayles' Brigade, Texas Militia.
>
> Senator Maetze represents the Twelfth Senatorial district, composed of the counties of Austin, Burleson, Washington, Waller and Fort Bend in the Twenty-first

---

22  Personnel of the Texas state government, with sketches of distinguished Texans, embracing the executive and staff, heads of the departments, United States senators and representatives, members of the Twenty-first Legislature : Daniell, L. E. (Lewis E.). Available at: https://archive.org/details/personneloftexas00dani2. Accessed September 8, 2017.

and Twenty-second sessions of the Texas Senate. In the Twenty-first session he served as chairman of the Committee on Rules and was a member of other important committees.

Senator Maetze has familiarized himself with the forms and fundamental principles of all governments, and is thoroughly acquainted with all the basic principles that underlie and give vitality to the institutions of this country. He is a prudent and safe legislator, and, having acquired a complete knowledge of the English language, he speaks with very slight accent, using chaste English with all the facility of an educated native.

He has been married twice, the first time in Germany in 1844, and the second time in 1860 in Texas.

Senator Maetze is a very striking man in personal appearance. He is of average height, slight with a very intelligent face and expressive features, with snow white hair and beard. His manners are dignified, but not austere. He is social and pleasant in society."

## *NAGEL*

*Charles Nagel*

Herman Nagel was a doctor from near Berlin. He and his wife emigrated in 1847, settling first on a small farm on the Bernardo Prairie. He soon resumed his medical practice, which he followed throughout his life. He moved his family to a small farm at Millheim in 1855. He strongly objected to Texas secession, and in 1863 fled with his son Charles to Mexico and ultimately reestablished in St. Louis, Missouri, where he was soon joined by the rest of his family. His son Charles became Secretary of Commerce and Agriculture under President William Taft, the first native-born Texan to be a member of a President's cabinet.

## REGENBRECHT

Adalbert Regenbrecht, son of a wealthy law professor and rector at the University of Breslau, emigrated in 1856 after obtaining his law degree. He boarded with E.G. Maetze and Dr. Nagel for a year, then bought a farm in Millheim. While his family continued to farm, he began professional work selling fire insurance.

## RINIKER

John Riniker was one of several from Canton Aargau, Switzerland who were recruited by Charles Amsler to come to Texas. They did so in 1851, settling near Millheim. He farmed and was a tailor of men's suits.

## ROMBERG

Johannes Christlieb Nathanael Romberg and his family emigrated from Rostock, Mecklenberg to Texas in 1847, settling on the Bernard three miles from Cat Spring. He was a prolific writer of poetry and is known as the German Poet Laureate of Texas. In 1853 they moved to Fayette County where he organized the Prairieblume Literary Society and wrote most of his poems.

*Johannes Christlieb Nathanael Romberg*

## SCHLUENS

Friedrich (Fritz) Schluens and his wife left Rostock settled near Millheim before 1850. He and his descendants have been instrumental in introducing Brahman cattle to this area. He was married to Marie A. Kloss in 1868. A street in Millheim is named after him where the historic Engelking Cemetery is located.

## SCHNEIDER

Wilhelm Schneider and family joined the Adelsverin-sponsored movement of Germans to Texas in 1846, but redirected to settle in Millheim instead of New Braunfels. Their son Carl came a year later. He later bought the Dr. Herman Nagel house when he left Texas during the Civil War, where he opened a general merchandise store.

## SEVERIN

John Severin, head of household, came from Germany to better their living conditions. Through other German emigrants they had heard of the beautiful hills, fertile valleys, abundance of wood and water in the Cat Spring-Millheim area and here they settled on a farm in 1867. Johann Severin was married twice and had eight children by his first wife, two of who, with their mother, Elizabeth, died in Texas frontier conditions. Otto A. Severin, a life long resident of Millheim and Bellville, was the only child by the second marriage to Minna Buescher Severin, born 1844 in Westphalia, Germany, died 1925 in Millheim, Texas.[23]

## SWEARINGEN

Elemelech Swearingen came from Holland to Pennsylvania, then Kentucky, then Texas in 1830. He first lived on a grant on Mill Creek, then moved to a small community that later came to be known as Clarksville, between Millheim and Cat Spring. He

---

23 Information supplied by Will Heaton.

fought at San Jacinto and was remembered as a close fiend of Sam Houston.

## TRENCKMANN

Andreas Friedrich Trenckmann ran a private school in Magdeberg. Siding with the losing side in the political disturbances of the 1840s, he emigrated with his family to Texas is 1853, settling first on the Bernard Prairie on land he purchased from noted Texas poet Johannes Romberg. In 1858 he bought a farm and gin in Millheim. He was an organizer and first president of the Cat Spring Agricultural Society. His youngest son William Andreas Trenckmann was valedictorian of the first graduating class of Texas A&M College, became a successful newspaper publisher in Bellville and Austin, and served in the Texas House of Representatives.

*William Andreas Trenckmann*

## VON ROEDER

Anton Ludwig Sigismund von Roeder was the head of a large aristocratic family that settled at Cat Spring in 1834.

The roots of the family are documented back to 1218[24] and extend back to the Carolingian and thus the Merovingian Dynasty.

He had been a high ranking nobleman and military officer in Prussia and was Feudal Baron of the estate at Hoym, Saxon-Anhalt. They had been attracted by a letter from Friedrich Ernst describing the land and opportunities there and it seems to be that he was in political trouble with the monarch. One of the

---

24  Von Roeder. Flora. *These are the Generations* Vol. 1, p. 4-5, CreateSpace, Charleston, 2012. Available at amazon.com.

legends around this is that one of his sons[25] had a duel with the kings's son[26] and killed him and the family only rescued him from execution (dueling was forbidden and a capital crime) by them forfeiting lands and property and going into exile.

He married Caroline Louise Sack with whom he had sixteen children and of whom eleven grew to maturity and ten emigrated to Texas[27]. Caroline was a member of the illustrious Sack Family mentioned elsewhere in this book and was at that time the wealthiest family in Prussia. It was also traditionally committed to education and financed the first public schools in Silesia.

Both the Sack and von Roeder families hold regular reunions both in Texas and in Germany to this day. The Sack Family also traces its origins back to the Merovingian Dynasty which gives them a strong sense of destiny – undoubtedly attributes which would act as drivers in building that new, better world in Texas.

Three von Roeder brothers (Louis[28], Albrecht[29] and Joachim[30]) and sister Valeska were sent ahead in the Spring of 1834 to secure a location for the others and to file land claims. Joachim and Valeska soon died of yellow fever. They first went to Industry by the earlier settlers, then to Cat Spring. Later the same year, Ludwig and his wife Caroline Louise Sack, their daughter Rosa and her new husband Robert Justus Kleberg, other daughters Louise and Caroline, sons Rudolph, William and Otto with wife Pauline and her sister Antoinette von Donop and Louis Kleberg made the journey to Texas and settled at Cat Spring.

---

25 J. Frank Dobie in *Tales of Old-Time Texas* (University of Texas Press Austin, 1983, p.173) attributes the story to Sigismund – although we do not have any record of a son with that name. In this version of the story, because the duel was fair, Sigismund was not sentenced to death but to life imprisonment. His son was released on the proviso that they leave Germany.

26 Or a lieutenant in the Prussian army according to Flora von Roeder (cf. http://www.cclibraries.com/localhistory/oldbayview/index.php/list-of-burials/622-otto-von-roeder. Accessed September 6, 2017).

27 Ibid, p.xi.

28 Carl Ludwig Socrates von Roeder.

29 Franz Ferdinand Albrecht Albert von Roeder.

30 Friedrich Anton Joachim Ludwig von Roeder.

Louis and Albrecht fought in the Texas Revolution serving in Capt. T.L. Parrott's Artillery Company. Louis von Roeder fought in the famous battle of San Jacinto[31]. He married Caroline Ernst von Hinueber[32]. For his services he received a league of land in Cat Spring[33]. The famous legend of the gambled bride is associated with Otto[34] von Roeder where he is supposed to have won a bride from a freshly wedded nobleman in a game of poker, whereupon Otto killed the contestant in self defense. According to this legend, Otto used the same sword as he had used to kill the prince in Prussia in a duel, mentioned above[35].

*VON WAMMEL*

Franz von Wammel came to Texas in 1845 and settled near Millheim. Originally a school teacher and musician, he farmed in Texas. He was a teamster hauling cotton to Mexico during the Civil War.

*VORNKAHL*

Johann Heinrich Vornkahl entered the United States on 10 Jan 1846 as stated in his letter of intent to file for citizenship (filed 12 Sep 1849). He was granted citizenship on 9 Nov 1853. - Henry Lee Vornkahl. He married Christine Maria Friederike

---

31  Ibid p. 37.
32  See page 181.
33  https://tshaonline.org/handbook/online/articles/frogt. Accessed September 4, 2017.
34  Frederick Arnold Otto Ludwig von Roeder.
35  See: Kearney, James C. Nassau Plantation: The Evolution of a Texas-German Slave Plantation, Univ of North Texas, 2011, p.30.

J. Frank Dobie in *Tales of Old-Time Texas* (University of Texas Press Austin, 1983, p.175) also attributes the story to a 'Sigismund' and the opponent was supposed to be a certain Benjamin Buckingham from who owned a plantation on the Brazos. We can only find a grandson Sigismund Arnold Theodor von Roeder born in 1832 and another named Sigismund Otto von Roeder born in 1848 (both too young to come into question for this story and the story about the duel!). The brides name was, according to this version, called Barbara Buckingham and was supposed to have married the Sigismund on the spot. There is no record of a spouse married to either of the Sigismunds with that name. So this story is very mixed up and difficult to verify. Apparently the tale was related to the author by Sigmund (Sigismund?) Engelking in 1951 in Comfort Texas, ibid p.324. This could be Sigismund Engelking Junior who died in 1956 in San Antonio who was born in Millheim in 1875.

*Johann Heinrich Vornkahl*

Perski. It seems they came from Hildesheim in Germany[36]. Like his ancestors, he too, as all persons in the world with the name "Vornkahl" originally came from one small village called Nettlingen near Hildesheim in Germany.

They initially lived in the Kleberg home until 1850 when he bought his own farm in the Millheim area:

"Enticed by freedom and open country, Heinrich Vornkahl left Germany and came to Texas, and the Vornkahl ranch began with approximately 150 acres that Heinrich purchased from David and Rebecca Portis in 1851. The founder was a member of the Cat Spring Agricultural Society and donated land for the Millheim Harmony Hall. He raised everything from pecans to corn, cotton, hay and silage, in addition to cattle and operating a dairy. Through the generations, the Vornkahl family moved into the business side of agriculture. For example, Walter Vornkahl, who inherited the ranch in 1923, managed a cotton gin in Millheim as well as a blacksmith shop and tractor repair service. He even assumed responsibility for Millheim school bus maintenance. Thanks to the hard work, through the generations, of families like the Vornkahls, Texas is the agricultural giant that it is today."[37]

---

36  Information from: http://www.vornkahl.net/famyli/vornkahl_deutsch.html. Accessed September 2, 2017.

37  Press release, Texas Department of Agriculture, Austin, Texas, March 5, 2002; *TDA to Honor Vornkahl Family Ranch at Family Land Heritage Ceremony*. cited in http://www.vornkahl.us/Pages%20529-650%20Sources%20-%202016%20final%20print.pdf. Accessed September 2, 2017.

There is a Historical Marker outside the current Millheim Harmonie Verein Hall. The Verein was officially organized in 1873 and its first elected officers were E.G. Maetze, President; W. Mersmann, Vice President; C. Schneider, Treasurer; and S. Engelking, Secretary. That hall was built in 1874 on two acres purchased from F. Engelking, Sr. and Heinrich Vornkahl.[38]

## *WELHAUSEN*

Carl Conrad Welhausen came to Cat Spring in 1843 to join friends who had earlier settled there, including the Amslers. His son Charles established a bank in Shiner. Their son Charles founded Tex Tan, the largest US saddle company, in Yoakum.

---

38 From: http://www.andrewbutlerphotos.com/p682672260/h8F9234F3#h8f9234f3. Accessed September 2, 2017.

# The Adolph Fuchs Family in Cat Spring

Ottilie Fuchs Goeth, member of the Adolph Fuchs family that lived in Cat Spring from 1846 to 1853, left for her children lengthy handwritten memoirs describing her life in Germany and continuing to her later years in Texas. Her granddaughter Irma Goeth Guenther translated these memoirs in 1969; they were published in a book titled *Memoirs of a Texas Pioneer Grandmother (Was Grossmutter Erzählt)*, published by Eakin Press in 1982. An early chapter in the book describes the Fuchs family's departure from Germany and their first eight years in Texas at Cat Spring[39].

Adolph Fuchs was a Lutheran minister in Kölzow, Mecklenberg, from 1835 to 1845. He and his wife Dorothea Margarete Schröder Fuchs had seven children when they emigrated in 1845.

Ottilie Fuchs said that her parents had discussed the idea of moving to America for some time before they told their children, who had begun instruction in English without knowing why. Their parents were preparing them for the move, knowing that they would need their help to survive in the new country. Adolph Fuchs joined the Adelsverein soon after it was organized, and began making plans to move to Texas. Finally, after a letter of acceptance was received, the children were informed of the move; they were ecstatic, running immediately to tell their

---

39  This book is available as a hard copy or in eReader format; it has also been reformatted in 2010 by Kenneth Fuchs and made freely available for reading on the internet: http://www.kenfuchs42.net/kfww/Ottilie%20Fuchs%20Goeth%20-%20Memoirs%20of%20a%20Texas%20Pioneer%20Grandmother.pdf,

friends. Fuchs followed detailed instructions provided by the Adelsverein as to what to bring, what crates to use, and other specifics.

Ottilie described her father's views regarding the reason for the move: "Father's dictum was, however, rather to earn a living by the sweat of his brow than be supported by the grace of God. Having to preach for a living was entirely contrary to his finer sensibilities. Had he been able to bring himself to make practical use of his musical and literary talents, there would have been no lack of the necessary income to raise his large family, even in comfortable circumstances. But perhaps he saw beyond all this with that certain clarity of vision, virtually inspired by divine providence." She went on to describe the oppressive conditions they experienced in Germany at that time that led two years later to the 1848 uprisings. Opportunities other than menial careers were hard to obtain, for girls and even young men who had obtained a college degree.

The Fuchs made extensive preparations for their journey. A dressmaker was employed for several weeks to make the required clothing. Her mother sold her finer dresses in favor of the more practical clothing to be worn in the "wilderness". Their furniture was sold. Fuchs delivered his farewell sermon to his congregation on November 11, 1845[40]. They traveled by train to Bremen, then Bremerhaven, where they boarded the ship Gerhard Hermann. Many of the ships then being used to transport Germans to Texas were old, weak, and poorly provisioned: "The old sailing vessels on which one came over from Bremerhaven were gruesome crates in comparison to the present elegant and comfortable steamships. One was at sea for ten to twelve weeks with horrible food and the worst imaginable drinking water." The Gerhard Hermann sank on its next trip to Galveston. They made a stop at Dartmouth, then proceeded

---

[40] The sermon was printed in a local newspaper; a copy brought to Texas by Fuchs was printed in a San Antonio newspaper in 1846, titled "Farewell to the Old World", a translation made by Lana Rings, PhD, is can be seen at https://adolphfuchs.wordpress.com/#translation . For additional information on Fuchs, see http://kenfuchs42.net/kfww_pastor_adolf_fuchs.html.

## The Adolph Fuchs Family in Cat Spring

across the Atlantic to reach Puerto Rico where they paused for a week, then went on to Galveston. Having learned of an outbreak of yellow fever in Indianola, their original destination, Fuchs decided to debark at Galveston and leave the Adelsverein program.

A small steamboat took them from Galveston to Houston; the voyage was pleasant and the food "excellent", at least compared to what they had eaten in the previous several weeks. A passenger on the steamboat gave Ottilie a pound of candy, which she "joyously divided among the children." They remained in Houston for eight days, then loading all their possessions on a wagon drawn by five pairs of oxen, they headed for Industry and Friedrich Ernst, who was already known as "'Father of the Emigrants, because of his generosity in advising and aiding everyone who sought him out." Ottilie marveled at how her mother was able to bake cornbread over an open fire as they crossed the huge expanse of prairie west of Houston. Male family members bagged deer and other game to add to the cornbread for their meals. Ottilie stated: "We were deeply impressed by the vastness of the prairies, endless as far as the eye could see. We were of course familiar with some large meadows, but these were always plotted out with ditches, while here the prairies appeared to dominate everything without barriers of any kind; all was free, the soil virtually begging for a hand to cultivate it."

They were impressed with the favorable reception they received on this leg of their journey: "I clearly remember the friendly reception we got from the Americans living along the main road, if one can so designate the path we traveled. Even today, Texas still has a reputation for hospitality, while it was all the more true at a period when every settler was received in almost festive fashion. Whatever they possessed was offered to the stranger with a certain irresistible charm. Racial prejudices did not yet exist. If the new arrival made an honest impression, it sufficed not to ask him about his forefathers." They arrived in Cat Spring in February, and decided to stay instead of going on to Industry. Ottile said: "Here we met the large families of the von Roeders, the sons-in-law of Mr. Kleberg; and the Engelkings, who had already resided there for thirteen years. All of these families received us with utmost friendliness, and they prevailed upon Father to establish his first home in Texas at Cat Spring."

They soon bought a small farm from the estate of a member of the von Roeder family, and immediately began planting crops with a small plough that had been left on the farm. Ottilie remembered her educated father, so unfamiliar with farming, behind the oxen pulling a plough: "How he must have suffered, this intellectual behind the plow; how clumsy and difficult it all was for the hands better suited to the use of a violin bow or at most a pair of light garden shears." Fortunately, a resident already familiar with the process rode by and stopped to show Fuchs how to handle the team and use the plough. They planted some fig trees that had been sent by Friedrich Ernst. Soon they developed close friendships with their neighbors. Things were different, but acceptable: "True, some conveniences were completely lacking and the more comfortable furnishings we previously had could not be replaced immediately. Still, everyone felt comfortable in our house as there was nothing better available elsewhere. The men sat outside under the oak trees; the women did not ask for upholstered chairs; a simple meal sufficed one, for every dish was well seasoned with Attic salt (charm, wit, intelligence), with gay and unfettered conversation, and lively discussions on art and literature. Although it may not have been the paradise we had visualized, it was a land of freedom where everyone was his own master."

The Fuchs family was very impressed by a barbecue celebration they attended in what later became the Bellville city park; this occurred in 1846, two years before the new county seat was founded. Traveling there across Mill Creek was a challenge: "Although we could see the houses in the vicinity of Bellville from our farm located fairly high on a hill, we had to travel for miles to reach the place. We had to detour through the impenetrably dark 'Millcreek Bottom' and then over prairies with thick grass, and wide-bladed grass reaching the chests of the horses. A path had to be hewn in order that the animals could get through.... The grounds where the celebration took place swarmed with black and white people. The wealthy slave holders, with their black servants were a unique sight for the Germans. I was only a child at the time, so I must have been all the more impressed by the strangeness of it. The official speaker was one General Portin[41]. His wife, a lady of considerable stature, like most of the other ladies, wore a muslin dress with large flowers printed upon it and fanned herself with an enormous spread of tail feathers from a turkey."

Ottilie Fuchs then described the large public barbecues that are still so revered and enjoyed by Austin County residents today: "At the Bellville celebration we also saw for the first time how large quantities of meat are roasted over open pits and then spread out on long tables for everyone to help themselves as desired. Later we attended other celebrations of this kind and became less aware of the uniqueness of the custom. Seeing young and old armed with huge chunks of meat which gradually disappeared into the mouth without ever having been cut, must have created great astonishment amongst us. Best I do not attempt to describe how we little ones coped with it. It must have been quite a sight."[42]

In 1847 the Kleberg and most of the von Roeder families moved to what became Meyersville, on a branch of Coleto Creek between Victoria and Cuero. The Fuchs family would have followed these friends to DeWitt County had not their oldest daughter Lulu, by then married to Wilhelm von Roeder, died of an acute fever. They remained in Cat Spring until 1853, then moving to a land grant in Burnet County near Marble Falls ob-

---

41  David Young Portis. His wife was the former Rebecca Cumings, finacee' of William Barrett Travis before his demise at the Alamo.

42  These large public barbecues continue to this day across Austin County, much as described here. Millheim has held it's annual Father's Day barbecue for over 80 years, and Cat Spring Agricultural Society held it's 161st annual June Fest barbecue in 2017.

tained by Fuchs before leaving Germany, to which he finally had received clear title. During his tenure in Cat Spring, Fuchs brought income to the family by teaching in the homes of wealthy plantation owners along the Brazos, and at the newly-established academy for women in Independence (later to become Baylor University).

The story of how Fuchs obtained this land was told by Ottilie as follows: "At the time we had decided to emigrate, a young man by the name of Hollin had returned to his home in Rostock from Texas in order to bring back a young bride from there. During this time, that is in 1844, some Texas land papers had been offered for sale in Mecklenburg at very low prices. Mr. Hollin had declared that land in Texas had no actual value as one needed only sufficient land for a house and fields, while there was free grazing land everywhere for the cattle. A number of these land papers were owned by Mayor Lüders in Marlow, who was a close friend of Father's. A brother of Mayor Lüders had been killed in Texas during the War of Independence. Anyone familiar with Texas history will recall that President Houston had to pay each soldier with a league of land because there was no money in the State Treasury. Lüders was also paid with a league of land which was turned over to his brother, the mayor, after his death. He first offered the papers to Mr. Hollin, who turned them down. Then when Mayor [Carl Friedrich Wilhelm] Lüders learned that his friend Pastor Fuchs was going to Texas, he said to him, 'Fuchs, would you like to have the papers? I will never have any use for them anyway. See that you get the land surveyed.' Father accepted the offer, whereupon the certificate was transferred to his name in Rostock. However, it took eight years, with numerous difficulties to overcome, before Father got possession of the land with aid of the land surveyor De Cordova. Had Father not been so fluent in English, we doubtlessly would never have gained possession of the land. One third of the land went to the surveyor, while the rest of it was surveyed for us at four different locations in the State. One section of 1,000 acres was located on the Clear Fork of the Brazos River, where the town of Lueders is located. Two other tracts of land of six hundred acres each were sold by Father at a very low price. He did not have any business ability whatsoever, otherwise he doubtlessly would have received a greater sum for the land." The Fuchs family remained on this land for the rest of their lives.

# The Cat Spring Agricultural Society

The oldest agricultural society in Texas is at Cat Spring. Its history was published by the society in 1956 as *Century of Agricultural Progress: 1856 - 1956*, and consists primarily of the minutes of the society carefully recorded and preserved over that time. The book's introduction, by W.N. Williamson, reads as follows:

"The Austin County Agricultural Society (Landwirthschaftlicher Verein) was organized June 7, 1856.

"The founders were well educated for that time, but knew very little about agriculture. Several were well trained in classical languages, music and literature, while others were technicians and craftsmen. They were often called "Latin Farmers." While they needed a great deal of guidance to make a living from the soil, such information was not readily available. It was necessary, therefore, that they form themselves into an agricultural society for mutual protection and benefit.

In answer to a call from a minister and a few others who were interested in the general welfare of the county the original meeting was held in the church. In their language the official title of this organization was Austin County Landwirth-shaftlicher Verein, which freely translated means the Austin County Agricultural Society. They drew up a constitution and 40 men indicated their interest and loyalty by signing it on June 7, 1856. Such signing was a requirement for membership. The purpose of this society, as stated in Article IV of the Constitution, was 'to develop an interest in agriculture and to solve related problems.' Action taken at the meeting was carefully recorded by the secretary.

"Until April, 1942 these minutes were written in German. Later minutes were written in English. Some of the early minutes are somewhat faded, though otherwise well preserved.

"The use of the German language in the Cat Spring community, both spoken and written, is gradually declining. In order to preserve and to acquaint future generations with the rich cultural background and the authentic agricultural history contained in these minutes, they have been translated into English. Every effort has been made to preserve the original meaning. This is emphasized by inserting an occasional German word in parentheses. Most minutes seem rather dry reading, but these are alive with a discussion of problems and happenings of the day and vibrate with human interest. They read like a story book.

"Early contact was made with the Patent Office and similar societies. ... It was agreed (in 1858) to inform the Patent Office that the Society was ready to accept the task and to make experiments proposed by the Department and to request the Department to furnish the necessary seeds.

"Problems grew directly out of the wants and needs of these German farmers. In most cases the people had to find answers to their own problems by pooling the best information then available. Members who had special training of any kind were expected to share this information with other members of the Society. The minutes of the seventh meeting state: 'Huber finished his discourse concerning the bee culture begun in the fifth meeting.'

"Among current problems recognized and discussed by the members of this society were:
　　The determination of a fair price for cotton ginning.
　　The best method of planting Irish potatoes
　　How to prevent prairie fires

Different methods of improving the soil

Simple method of making cheese and necessary refreshments

The suitability of wild grapes and fruit for making wine

Seed treatment for disease control

Soil building practices

Method of seedbed preparations

"Recognition of problems implies a previous analysis of the situation even though no mention is made in the minutes of any particular analysis as such. By modern standards their methods of program building may appear crude but the results, though sometimes incomplete, were highly satisfactory at the time. These early planners can be credited with using al of the necessary elements of agricultural program building in their planning procedure.

"Except for a three-year interruption during the Civil War, this agriculture society has held regular monthly meetings and one annual meeting from the day of its organization to the present time. After 100 years the society has not lost sight of its original function, but the emphasis has been redirected.

"The social aspect had a definite place in the early meetings. At least once a year, usually on July 4, the Society held a big celebration principally for members and their families. Guests were invited only if the host would be responsible for their behavior. Plans were made for one of these July 4th celebrations at the 245th meeting held May 23, 1858. A committee was designated to work out the rules and regulations for the celebration, and to buy a United States flag. By general agreement the band was to 'play from noon until the early the next morning, or as long as the management permits.'"

Williamson concludes his introduction with recognition of the three men who translated the minutes: A.L. Schutte (1856 - 1882), E.P. Krueger (1882 - 1914) and E.A.. Miller (1914 - 1942).

Although most of the farming topics and techniques discussed were scientifically sound and obviously helped improve the farm and ranch yield, a few entries were clearly in the "folk remedy" category. From the 1850s and 1860s:

"For 'quinsy' (an infection of the tonsils in swine) it is recommended to heat a nail until red and then drill a hole with it through the skin at the throat. It will help almost immediately.

"A bottle of whiskey and a bottle of warm milk were recommended by some members for stock passing blood in the water, to be given once, twice, or as often as necessary.
"As a remedy against "flaps" (a mouth disease among cattle) Mr. Sens reported that he had used with success chimney soot, salt, and alum. He used salt and soot in the same proportions, but a little less of the alum. He rubbed the tongue of the sick animal until it bled.

"Mr. Bergmann declared that 'lock-jaw' among horses can be cured with chloroform. The chloroform is poured on a rag which is held against the nose of the afflicted animal until it breaks down. If a pistol is held between the ears of the afflicted animal and fired, this will also give the desired results.

"It is believed that the moon has great influence on plant and animal life. Fresh meat and fish caught will spoil almost immediately when exposed to the moon light. Calves should be branded or castrated during a declining moon.

"If cattle become badly infested with warts, they should be given three or four tablespoons of sulphur every 14 days until they disappear." The warts or the cows?

Several new plant species were introduced to the area by the society, including the Osage Orange tree, better known as Bois d'Arc or 'bodark'. On March 4, 1860, "Mr. Himley gave his long promised lecture on the culture of Bois d'Arc for hedges. Debates followed. Young Bois d'Arc plants can be obtained from Schluens on the old Crump's place in Ruterville and from

Walker's place at Frelsburg." Descendants of these imported trees are commonly seen in Austin County today.

One of the founders of the Cat Spring Agricultural Society in 1856, Louis Constant, became a pariah to the Society three years later when he openly opposed a letter sent by the Society to Germany encouraging more immigration. Constant sent an article to the Koeniglich Privelegierte Berlinsche Zeitung (Royal Privilege Berlin Daily News) that was written on June 15, 1858, published on August 4, 1858, and reads in part as follows: "The Agricultural Society of this county has released an article to several newspapers in Germany for the purpose of promoting the immigration into Texas. I am informed that my name is listed as one of the signature to that article. The article in question may likely have been endorsed by certain individuals. It was, however, not submitted to me for review, and I am therefore, and herewith severing my relations to them. Condonement would also involve my moral responsibility to possible emigrants who respond to that article.

"Texas is the land of anomalies and irregularities; because not only the humans follow very peculiar paths, but also the physical world pleases to indulge in singular caprices and contrasts! The past seven years have visited us with ice and snow at a time of the year when warm spring winds are wafting already in Germany; then followed drought and heat, and consequently the cash tills were rather empty in fall. Scanty existence here, but real want, scarcity of feed and lack of water have occurred in other places, so that an estimated number of 40,000 head of horned cattle in all may have perished. Amidst all this comes the exhortation, 'Come to Texas!'

"Here we are really experiencing contrasts! With the late winter came thunderstorms, and floods of water poured down on the earth. The roads were turned into bottomless morass and freight traffic ceased to function. Food prices rose to almost unbelievable heights: three dollars for a bushel of corn, which normally costs 50c. Entire counties have requested credit from the government to even enable them to buy the needed seed corn. In spite of all this they shout, 'Come to Texas!'

Constant goes on to begrudgingly admit that the health conditions of the area were favorable. He also gives a jaded view of the people who had settled in Texas, including his German neighbors, and accuses the Agricultural Society to be "the handiwork of a single individual (unnamed but presumably Rev. Bergmann), approved by a few individuals, and the mass of the members were used simply as a foil." Constant accused the society of promoting more immigration as a means of gaining additional low-cost labor for their farms. His accusation was at least in part correct because many of the new immigrants spent their first years in Texas working as laborers for an existing farmer. However, after a few years of this labor, many of the newcomers saved enough money to buy their own land and become independent farmers themselves, something that few could hope to accomplish in Europe. Even before Constant wrote his letter to the German newspaper the report and his views were discussed by the society. Rev. Bergmann introduced the subject on February 21, 1858; he read a report prepared by a committee on the promotion of immigration to East Texas. On April 25, 1858 the society voted to remove Constant's name from the immigration document, and on May 23, 1858, he was expelled from the society by a vote of 28 for and 22 against. One might detect a hint of revenge over his actions regarding his June 15th letter. Evidently relations improved because on September 3, 1865, the society voted that the original resolution banning Constant from membership be rescinded. Although Constant was viewed as a visionary and promoted making Constant Creek (named after him) navigable through Mill Creek and the Brazos to the Gulf of Mexico, thus creating Millheim as a port, he eventually had his fill of Texas and returned to Germany.

# The Millheim Harmonie Verein

The history of this society was published in their *Centennial Celebration of Millheim Harmonie Verein* in 1972. Henry Ripple translated the minutes of the society and from them prepared the following history.

"It was some time after this (the Civil) war and the Reconstruction Period that followed before things became normal again. It was during this period that the citizens of this community felt the need of having an organization to carry on the German tradition as well as a place for entertainment and social activities, and the Millheim Harmonie Verein was formed for the enjoyment and benefit of its members, their families and friends.

"In this first General Assembly at Millheim, Texas held on August 30 (1872) at the old school house the name "Millheim Harmonie Verein" was chosen by the newly founded organization. The installed officers were as follows: E.G. Maetze as President, Wilhelm Mersmann, Sr. as Vice-President, Chas. Schneider, treasurer, and Sigismund Engelking as Secretary. ...

"In the first general meeting it was disclosed that a drive would be made to get new members and in a later meeting a Community Program was prepared for the Millheim School Precinct. The early meetings were held every month beginning at 8:00 p.m. sharp. The membership fees were $5.00 per year and new members had to be 18 years of age. The first dance was held on February 28, 1873. Dance tickets were 25c for men. ...

"On July 3, 1874 a special meeting was called at which time it was decided to build a hall. The size was 30' x 52' and 14' high. Lumber at that time cost $20.00 per 1000 (board) foot. Messers F. Engelking, Sr. and Heinrich Vornkahl offered two acres of land to the society at $15.00 per acre upon which to build the hall. The site was selected as it was near the home of Herbert Goller and his wife. He operated a small brewery and bowling alley which no doubt offered an additional attraction.

"The old Harmonie Hall served the Verein and its members for many years and was the center of social activities in Millheim. It is the place where the Singing Society met and the Agricultural Society had their meetings. It was used for political rallies and to hold elections. The annual barbecue was held here, the Maifest, Christmas Tree Dance, New Year's Ball, Annual Masquerade Ball and Leap Year Dance. It was also the place of family gatherings, school programs, wedding anniversaries, etc. ...

"In 1938 a special meeting was held at which time it was decided by the members that the old hall had served its purpose. There was no room for expansion, the hall was in need of repairs which were prohibitive, so it was decided to build a new hall on a tract of land offered to the Verein by Mr. Otto Severin, who was a member in long standing. This is the present location. The old hall was torn down and what lumber could be used was salvaged and used in the new building. ... All of the new members as well as some of the old ones volunteered their services and the work was done by the members free of charge. ... The first dance in the new hall was held on April 15, 1939."

Today the major annual event is the Father's Day barbecue, in an air conditioned hall, featuring live music and a traditional cakewalk as well as outstanding meat — beef, pork and mutton, cooked on large open pits — and all the trimmings.

# The Millheim Land Swindles

One of the most extensive court cases involving disputed land claims in Texas took place in Austin County and involved many of the early Millheim settlers. William Heaton, who owns land in the formerly disputed area inherited from his great-grandfather Johan Serverin, has extensively researched the deed records and their related litigation history. It is an extremely convoluted and fascinating, legal and multiple entwined family dispute that lasted for nearly 30 years. The following is a summary of Heaton's research.

The story begins with the arrival of the Cumings family to Austin's Colony in early 1822. Family matriarch Rebekah Cumings and her three sons John, James, and William, and daughter Rebecca were awarded a five league land grant of 22,140 acres, called a "hacienda" and later known as the Mill Tract. It extended from the lower reaches of Mill Creek near its mouth on the Brazos, upstream on both sides for eight miles to end southwest of Bellville. The Cumings had operated a mill in their former home in Kentucky. The uniquely large grant was given in recognition of the importance of this mill to the nascent colony's development; boards to build homes in San Felipe were sawed here, and corn was ground into meal. Rebecca became the finacée of William Barret Travis but this relationship died with him in the Alamo. James died in 1825 without a will, but not before he had "sold" the middle two leagues of the Mill Tract to James E.B. Austin, brother of Stephen, without proper title transfer. William and John each owned the outer two 1.5

leagues of the Mill Tract. When William died in 1828, his widow and only son Samuel went back to Kentucky. When John died in 1839 with no heirs, his estate was awarded to Rebecca.

When Stephen Austin died in 1836, his will left half of his estate to his sister Emily Perry and the other half to his nephew and namesake Stephen, son of James E.B. Austin and wife Eliza Martha Westall Austin, as long as he lived. Unfortunately young Steven soon died, and Emily claimed the entire Austin estate including the middle two leagues in the Mill Tract. Martha remarried lawyer William Green Hill. Soon after her son's death they decided to claim ownership of the half of Stephen Austin's estate that was left to her son in Austin's will, despite the clause that clearly left it to Emily Perry when young Stephen died. A lawsuit was filed in 1838 by the Perrys against the Hills concerning the half of the Austin estate left to young Stephen. It wound its way to the Texas Supreme Court until it was finally resolved in 1842 with a settlement that awarded the two middle leagues of the Mill Tract being awarded to the Hills.

Meanwhile, Rebecca married David Young Portis, fourteen years her junior, in 1843. He was a prominent lawyer in San Felipe and one of the richest men in Austin County and a Republic of Texas Senator. He had moved here in 1839 to escape a debt owed in Alabama; he went by the title "General" although he never saw military service. He promptly took over management of Rebecca's land holdings, and claimed that she owned all five leagues of the Mill Tract, ignoring the James Cumings "sale" of the middle two leagues to Austin and the 1842 decision awarding it to the Hills, the fact that the William Cumings 1.5 league share was clearly inherited by his son Samuel in Kentucky, and Rebecca's still uncertain title to the lower 1.5 leagues.

During all the legal wranglings of ownership of the Mill Tract, David Portis had sold tracts to several of the German immigrants in Millheim. At that time David and Rebecca Portis were living nearby on Mill Tract land.

Further complicating the legal land title mess, Samuel Cumings returned to Texas in 1848 to claim his inheritance of the upper league and a half, which by that time was claimed by Portis, who had already sold much if it to others. The Hills filed a lawsuit contesting the entire ownership of the Mill Tract five leagues against Portis and Samuel Cumings. The Germans who had bought land from Portis in the disputed area were named as defendants in the lawsuit. It was, to put it mildly, a real mess!

The Hill v. Portis lawsuit was finally decided by the Texas Supreme Court in 1868 and awarded the middle two leagues of the Mill Tract to the Hills, the upper 1.5 leagues to Samuel Cumings, and split ownership of the lower 1.5 leagues between Cumings, his heirs, and Portis. The Millheim Germans who had bought land in the Mill Tract from Portis or from those who did so summarily lost title to their land without compensation. Many later redeemed them from Samuel Cumings, and remained in the area, allowing the Millheim community to thrive.

Those Millheim settlers who lost title to their land because of the lawsuit included: William Schneider, Sr. and Jr., C. Wommoh, Christian Kramar, Rudolph Goebel, Franz Von Wammel, Emil Kloss, Charles Schneider, John Reineke, Louise Kleberg, William Mersmann, F. Tondike, Johann Vorbreck, Albert Hagemann, Louis Constant, Gustav Mateze, Louis Julius Wilson, William Keuffel, Jules Necker, George Plumsky, Jules Goebel, Fredrick Amsler, H. Bolten, Heinrich Vornkahl, Marcus Amsler, and Dehap Matthews.

# Pioneer Times at the A. and M.

## WILLIAM TRENCKMANN 1878

In comparison with the Paleozoic age and the time taken up in waiting for connections at Milano Junction, thirty years isn't so very long, but long enough to acquire considerable experience and an interesting family in passing through them. If the devoted student of the A. and M. of this day wishes to realize how far 1876 lies back, he has only to recall that when the doors of this, the first of all the State schools for higher education, were thrown open, deer in numbers still ran unmolested over the College prairies; that in the fall of 1876 the scream of the puma or Mexican lion frequently startled the sentries on the lower floor of the Main Building from their dreams "of pleasures that waited on life's merry morn," and an unlimited supply of "cush"; that baseball was then in its infancy in Texas, football had never been heard of, and no college yell had yet been composed. Then will he realize that one who can talk of the early days from personal experience must be old enough to be a grandfather. If the mists of thirty years obscure the dark shadows and help to give a rosy hue to events that had a deeper tinge at their occurrence, so much the better, for, as I understand it, the Long Horn wants "reminiscences", and not a chronicle.

I am not sure whether it was on the last Saturday in September, 1876, or the first Saturday in October, when, from a window of a Central passenger coach, the Main Building, the old Mess Hall and a row of two-story brick houses erected to accommodate the professors and their families, first loomed up before my expectant gaze. Passenger trains moved more slowly then, and the trip from Hempstead had seemed an age to my youthful imagination. No devoted crusader ever hailed the sight of the Holy City with greater joy than I felt, when those buildings on the bald College prairie arose before me. Just then the vision was partly obscured by a phenomenon that, as far as my memory reaches back, had not been seen before in Texas. Great clouds of grasshoppers that had devoured the grain of Kansas, in their flight southward hid the bright autumn sun; they covered the track, the wheels were slipping, and the engineer had to throw wide open the throttle to keep the train in motion, and in a few minutes the College was left far behind and I had to disembark in Bryan. There I was told that the College wagon would probably come in soon. But that wagon, drawn by a span of big mules, did not show up in Bryan till late on Sunday — it was the longest Sunday of all my life — to carry me and a load of groceries to the College. I got there all right, and half an hour later I was profoundly sorry for it, and longed for nothing so much as for the old farm in Millheim and a stout hoe-handle. Supper over, I found myself the center of attraction for some twenty young Texans, between fifteen and twenty-five, who had arrived during the preceding week, had witnessed the opening exercises, listened to noble oratorical effort by the great men of Texas; and then, to pass the time, set out to do a little hazing that would have made a West Pointer green with envy. That the long, lank, raw-boned youth from Austin County, who hadn't had a chance to speak English for months and years, formed an inviting subject for their efforts, is easily understood.

What happened that night in the Main Building to the latest arrival has, as I have been informed, furnished the theme for some excellent banquet stories, and I am not going to spoil them by giving my own recollections. Suffice it to say that I was "initiated" to the "queen's taste," and that, when I finally fell into a troubled sleep, my opinion of those fine young fellows who had greeted me so cordially had fallen to a zero point, and I had made up my mind to use the muscle acquired in exercises with maul and axe on anybody who might try to put me on guard duty again. But that never became necessary; it seems that I had not stood the test so badly, and next morning I was well acquainted and at home at the A. and M. College of Texas.

Monday morning, bright and early, we took possession of the Main Building, which was to be our dormitory. Matriculation over, roommates were selected, quarters chosen, an attempt at classification made, and "rules and regulations" read that sounded as severe as the code of Draco. In the afternoon Major Morrill, the commandant, gave us an insight into the military feature by drilling the awkward squad. The Major was martial from the word "go." Although rather small in stature, his voice sounded clear across the campus, which at that time extended to the railroad tracks.

The Major had evidently made up his mind that A. and M. cadets should soon set an example to those of his Alma Mater, the Virginia Military Institute. Setting-up exercises, marching single file with raw recruits who tread on each others' heels, etc., are not so very funny, as "Fish" of modern times will testify; but we had a good drill-master, who soon brought order out of chaos. My military career was destined to be brief, for the Major soon discovered in which direction my talents did not lie, and after I succeeded in leading the left wing of the battalion into a ditch at the Volksfest at Houston, in May, 1877, I was made quartermaster, and could watch the beautiful wheels and the soul-stirring bayonet exercises and artillery drills in which the Major delighted, or go botanizing in the dewberry patches — side-tracked on the road to martial fame, and yet the envy of many.

The teachers make the school, so we must take a glance at the faculty which, however, deserves more than a glance, for it consisted of men not easily to be forgotten. At the head President Gathright, an intimate of the great leader of the "Lost Cause"; a college man, and yet a soldier in his bearing, whose mien and voice called for unquestioning obedience. Though past middle age, his temper was fiery, but he possessed, withal, a kind heart. In addition to these qualities, he had a rich store of knowledge and a scorn of everything mean, untruthful, or ungentlemanly. Sometimes erred, but when he did he made amends lavishly. Many of the lectures he delivered to the students in the old chapel (now Professor Giesecke's realm) have proven an inspiration to us all. Their burden always was: "Whatever you be, whatever you do, be a man, be a gentleman." Dr. Martin, Doctor of Theology, and deeply versed in Latin and Greek, was chaplain and teacher of Science. His hair was gray, his honors and his years many, and he labored faithfully for our spiritual welfare. He tried his best to harmonize the views of a strict Presbyterian of the older days with the teaching of modern science; and if his instruction was mostly theory and no practice, it is to be remembered that such was the rule then, and that practically there were no appliances, no apparatus to work with. Some of his students in Chemistry, however, succeeded in making the section room, and even the entire Main Building, uninhabitable with sulphureted hydrogen and chlorine gas on several occasions. The chair of Modern Languages was held by Major Banks, big in body, big of heart, gentle and kindly, and ready to give help and fatherly advice to all. It was a pleasure to know Major Banks, and his memory will live until all the pioneer A. and M. cadets have answered the last roll-call. If the younger generation of Texans in those days were considered rather uncouth, "wild and woolly," by the outside world, no better model could have been selected for us than Professor Hand, who occupied the chair of Ancient Languages, beside whom even Lord Chesterfield would have appeared a veritable boor. His politeness, however, was not only an outward gloss, but it came from a kind and generous soul. Professor Alexander Hogg and Major R.P.W. Morris, whose spheres were Pure Mathematics and Applied Mathematics, respectively, alone of this first faculty are still in the land of the living, and I will spare their modesty by omitting the encomiums which they well deserve. Both are well known to the world; Professor Hogg as an ardent advocate of industrial progress, Major Morris by his participation in the political affairs of his native state. All were men if high standing in their chosen profession, perhaps the strongest and best informed that could have been selected in the Southland. The fact, however, that most of them before they came to Texas had been at the head of educational institutions, bore within it the seed of discord which, fortunately, did not germinate until after my time. Today a professor or an instructor at the A. and M.

College must be a specialist in some particular line, always striving to excel in that line. Then it was different; for the school was an agricultural and technical training school in name only; it was a literary institution mainly, and as such it soon took high rank, for certainly it could not have been the good looks and brass buttons of its students alone which within a single year made it the most popular school in Texas.

And now, as to the students. They had come from the farthest confines of Texas, east and west, north and south, and from many different walks of life.

Some were the sons of lawyers, merchants, ministers, and teachers, and had enjoyed the best training that our higher schools then afforded. Some were sons of farmers and ranchmen, and more at home in the saddle than in a section room. Some were mere striplings, others well advanced in years and tired and tested in the storms of life. Take them all in all (pardon me if this sounds boastful), they were as fine an aggregation of young Texans as one might wish to see, though by no means inclined to grow pale and haggard with overmuch study. From week to week their number increased. Perhaps fifty went home on furlough in the first Christmas vacation. Seventy came back. At the beginning of the second term in February the number had increased to one hundred and thirty, and the upper stories of the Old Mess Hall had to be used as a dormitory. When the second session opened, we were literally "as thick as three in a bed," and in the crush and jam at the beginning of that session, trying to find a bunk for everyone, fitting two hundred and sixty cadets of all sizes and proportions into as many uniforms ordered without measurement. I learned that even a quartermaster's occupation wasn't altogether a sinecure. Wooden barracks were hastily erected, a big two-story box house, and in the upper story of this makeshift structure I roomed for a year with Captain Sleeper, whom I followed as a shadow.

Early in the first session, the Stephen F. Austin Literary Society was organized, and the debates and oratory made the "welkin ring" with the recital of patriotism and glory of Spartacus, Mark Anthony, and Patrick Henry. The Society grew and prospered, until out of prosperity arose jealousy, and finally secession. The Calliopean Society came into being, rivalry between the two societies was keen, and great were the joint debates at Commencement.

The rapid increase in attendance brought with it other troubles than lack of room and overwork for the teachers. Many parents imagined that military discipline at the A. and M. would prove a cure-all for wayward sons, and many of the latter came with their minds set on getting just as much fun as possible out of their banishment. Major Morris and his successor, Captain Olmstead, of the United States Army, had their hands full in trying to control these young rebels. Strict regulations only added zest to their violation, and stolen excursions at night were all the more delightful when all the floors were guarded by sentries with fixed bayonets. A lightening rod furnished the means of escape from the fourth stoop. Gambling and drinking cropped out, and it was only by the united efforts of the faculty and the more thoughtful students that a better spirit got the upper hand. The student officers, especially, were in a trying position, for young men who had not learned to respect parents or teachers at home, were reluctant to obey orders from fellow-students wearing the stripes of corporal, sergeant, or other officer. Finally the precedent was set and the rule established that certain differences between officers and privates were not to be taken before the commandant, but must be settled according to the primitive method in an honest fist fight, and while this was not strictly military, results were quite satisfactory.

The "grub" question is likely to be an interesting one to students at all times, and I must say a few words about the Mess Hall. General H.P. Bee, the gallant soldier and dignified Southern gentleman, was in charge, and, if I mistake not, our young appetites came near bankrupting this generous man, who gave the best he had without carefully figuring out the profits. His noble wife appeared as an angel of mercy by her motherly visits to many a poor, lonesome cadet, who lay in his room ill and homesick at the same time. After General Bee came Mr. Sbisa, and Sbisa it has been to this day. That neither Bee nor Sbisa ever succeeded in satisfying all demands I need hardly tell, for college boys have always been "kickers," and probably will continue so to the end of time.

Many were the mess hall rebellions and numerous squibs and innuendos directed at the mess hall fare in the "Collegian."

In the line of amusements there was a little baseball, foraging expeditions into rural districts and surroundings on Saturdays, stag dances and debates on Saturday nights, now and then a concert or circus in Bryan, a fire alarm at night, the Commencement ball, and the never-to-be-forgotten April Fool's day. The long excursions on foot into the wildwoods of Brazos County, with a possum hunt and a chicken dinner as crowning the event, and the glorious comradeship which the very isolation of the school helped to develop, are to me cherished remembrances.

A thousand happenings, amusing or sad, and often a blending of fun and sadness, I can recall and might relate; and I believe that General Rogan wouldn't mind now if I told about that "kangaroo court," or about good old Dr. Martin granting full pardon to those who turned his shed bottom side up, long before he went to his last reward. But I have already taken up too much space in telling of these old times to those who live in the new. May the dear old A. and M. prosper and expand in its great work for Texas!

W.A. Trenckmann, Class of 1879

*From the 1907 Long Horn (Texas A&M's yearbook), Pages 112-113.*

# Christmas in Troubled Times

## William A. Trenckmann

Translated by
ANDERS SAUSTRUP

## Translator's Preface

William Andreas Trenckmann was a settled man of 34, married and father of three, when he wrote this memoir of a Texas-German Christmas. Two years earlier, in 1891, and with only two paid subscriptions in hand, he had started Das Bellville Wochenblatt, a weekly newspaper published in Bellville, Texas and intended for the neighboring Texas-German communities in which English was still a second language. Trenckmann was born about ten miles from Bellville in one of those communities, Millheim, in 1859, the son of immigrant German parents. Becoming a newspaperman and printer had meant abandoning a rewarding common-school teaching career, which he had pursued for a number of year—in Frelsburg, Shelby (Rodersmuhl), and Bellville—after attending Texas A&M College where he had arrived on horseback in the fall of 1876, when A&M first opened its doors.

The *Bellville Wochenblatt* was a successful gamble. After eighteen years, during four of which (1905-1909) he represented his district in the Texas House of Representatives, Trenckmann moved his family and enterprise, now called simply Das Wochenblatt, to the state capital where it was published until 1933 when he sold it, after editing it for a total of forty-two years. For a few years during the 1890's Trenckmann maintained the practice of issuing free supplements to his paper in the form of an almanac, Kalender, for the upcoming year. In 1899, however, he was much more ambitious and produced a booklet, *Austin County: Beilage zum Bellville Wochenblatt, den alten Texanern gewidmet und den jungen Texanern zu Nutz und Frommen*, really the first attempt at a topographical and historical account of a county which was the seat of Stephen Austin's colony and the site of the first German settlement in Texas. In the very first of these supplements, few copies of which have survived, the *Wochenblatt Kalender fuer 1894*, we find the present memoir, Eine Weihnachtsfeier trüber Zeit.

The setting is the community of Millheim on Mill Creek in Austin County, where a number of Germans had settled in the 1840's and '50's in reaction to their political and economic frustrations in Germany. Some half-dozen Texas-German settlements, Millheim one of them, have been nicknamed Latin Settlements because many of their residents were men previously engaged in intellectual and academic pursuits, who had now chosen to learn, mostly from books, how to tend land and make a raw living in the New World where they could call themselves free. As might be expected, many of their efforts on Mill Creek, even under wilderness conditions, were directed towards self-improvement and education.

At the meetings of Cat Spring landwirtschaftlicher Verein (Agricultural Society), of which William Trenckmann's father was the first President in 1856 — its minutes were kept in German language until 1942 — bookish would-be farmers shared trials and errors. But the true pride of the community was its school, first at the Sigismund Engelking[43] home, later, after a fire, even outdoors, with the children sitting on tree stumps under the energetic tutelage of Ernst Maetze, a graduate of the University of Breslau and former member of the Frankfurt Parliament.

---

43 This was actually the home of Ferdinand Engelking, father of Sigismund.

As the Civil War drew closer and finally broke out, these struggling, high-principled Texas-Germans were confronted with political and moral dilemmas beyond their comprehension and seemingly without solution: though opposed to slavery, would they still not have to accept that Texas—one of only three of the eleven states of the Confederacy to have a referendum on the matter—by majority vote had chosen to secede from the Union? Or should they put personal principle and conviction above community decision when an immoral cause was pursued? The Christmas memoir tells us what they did in actual practice. Friends and neighbors were divided; there were splits within families; some who remained loyal to their personal convictions fled to Mexico, while others felt equally obligated to serve in the Confederate Army. Though a mere child at the time of the actual events, the memory of the dilemma of his parents' generation stayed with Trenckmann throughout his life. It is no doubt due to this influence that the *Wochenblatt*—a small newspaper read only by a linguistic minority—for almost half a century spoke in a firm and steady voice against the aberrations of the new as well as the old country, be it the Ku Klux Klan or, when the editor was an old man, emerging Nazi Germany.

I owe thanks to Margaret Woodruff for assistance with the translation and to the Peaceable Kingdom School for acts of kindness during the preparation of this English version of W. A. Trenckmann's Christmas Memoir, which is affectionately dedicated to his descendants.

## Christmas Memoir

It's strange how human memory works! Many experiences which at one time made our hearts beat more joyfully or tremble in pain—experiences we thought would be stamped on our minds forever—become indistinct and are finally altogether erased by the multitude of impressions produced by every single day; whereas other experiences, which we may anxiously endeavor to forget, seem ineradicable, as if carved in stone, and appear before our minds' eye in the sleepless hours of the night or the hustle and bustle of the day. Events significant and worthy of note are often quickly forgotten, while those insignificant and objectionable are faithfully preserved. I have been told by people who are well on in years that in advanced age the happenings of earliest childhood are recalled all the more vividly, though the occurrences of the present are already covered by the veil of oblivion in a matter of hours and days.

In my case, as probably in the case of many another of my readers, the earliest distinct memory is associated with Christmas. If I now intend to try to evoke this memory and dress it in words as vividly as possible, then I do so chiefly with the intention of making possible a comparison between the much-praised good old days and the frequently scorned present.

In recent weeks, in conversation with heads of families, I have quite often heard the statement, "Times are too bad and money is too scarce; there of no way we can think of having a merry Christmas". As if the joy of celebration depended on the quantity and the monetary value of the gifts, rather than on the spirit of love with which they are chosen and given to our little ones.

Nowadays it is made so easy even for people without means (fortunately we don't as yet have real poverty out here in the country) to make their children happy at Christmas. In all districts of Germany, in France and Switzerland, in far-off Japan and the United States, thousands of wise minds are thinking, hundreds of thousands of diligent hands are stirring, year in and year out, in order to produce a thousand different kinds of more or less valuable objects, which are intended for the sole purpose of delighting the little ones of all nations.

Things were different thirty years ago, at the time into which I would like to project my readers in spirit. Back then there truly was no money in circulation, with the exception of worthless paper money which no one wanted to accept; and even those few who still were in possession of good money were not even able to use it to purchase those things that we today consider to be necessities of life, and much less articles of luxury or even toys. In such a situation it was only the all-conquering, sacrificing love on the part of fathers and mothers which, even in the days of severe distress, managed to preserve the beautiful customs of the old German homeland; which made them forget distress and misery and brighten the gloomy days for their children with the glimmering of the Christmas tree.

Christmas of 1863! — that was perhaps the very most troubled point in time of that terrible period in which the disastrous fraternal war was raging, transforming one part of the sunny South into a wilderness and the rest into a great house of mourning. After the battles of Gettysburg and Vicksburg, not only the expectation of a victory for their cause, but also the hope of an acceptable settlement had vanished even on the part of the most zealous Southern Bourbons. The flower of Southern manhood had fallen on the blood-drenched fields of Virginia and at Gettysburg or ended up imprisoned in the North; and whoever did not deliberately keep his eyes closed, had to recognize clearly that all martial art of the Southern military leaders, all the heroic courage of the Southern soldiers, were futile in the face of the inexhaustible resources of the North and would prolong a struggle that had no prospects. But even in the hearts of those who cherished no sympathy for Secession, no cheerful feelings could be aroused. Persecuted by the hate of the zealous secessionists and described as traitors, they were hovering in constant danger and saw ruination before their eyes, however the fortunes of war might turn.

The situation was saddest of all in the German settlements of our state. In most cases the settlers had been in the country for only a few years and had but limited means; for that reason they could not pay for a substitute, as did the rich slave owners. At the very beginning of the war a few had fled across the Mexican border or to the North, so that they would not have to join the Southern army; still others had gone to war, either of their own free will or under duress, leaving wife and child helpless and without protection. Others instead were hiding out in the bushes and ventured home only at night by devious routes, in order not to fall into the hands of the zealous conscriptors, who were hunting draft evaders everywhere. As a result of the iron belt of the blockade, the South was now entirely cut off from the world. Food supplies, items of clothing, even drugs were either not to be had at all or at best only at prices that were almost impossible. The fields had been tilled in a makeshift manner by women and children, or were lying completely fallow. Mourning, Worry, Fear, or Dire Need—these had made themselves at home in every house.

Nor was the house of my parents spared by these ugly guests. My father, to be sure, was too old to be drafted, but since all his sons were in the field, he had been forced to lease his gin, mill, and farmland as well. My oldest brother who already had a family of his own, had been taken prisoner at Vicksburg and was now waiting somewhere in Ohio to be released. My brother Otto was in winter quarters with Sibley's brigade in Louisiana and did not seem to have lost his good spirits. Brother Hugo was in a swampy camp on the Texas coast, and for months already our brother Adolph, dashing and always cheerful, had been sleeping the sleep of the dead on a Virginia battlefield. All that was known at the time was that the larger part of his regiment had been mowed down while storming the enemy position. His name was, however, not on the list of the fallen, and thus in their hearts our parents could still nourish the hope that he might have been captured, and they continued to hope for news of him. It never came, this news so eagerly awaited. That was the darkest shadow hovering over my parents' house at the time—Our queer daredevil cousin—or rather uncle Hermann, who, being a German subject, had joined the great war just for the fun of it, was at home recovering from a bullet through his cheek, a wound in his leg, and the hospital fare. He was already hobbling around rather nimbly on a crutch, entertaining everybody within reach with his war experiences, and when every once in a while a battle report arrived, he would complain loudly about not having been there.

Whether joy or sorrow prevails in the hearts of men, whether tranquil peace or war and pestilence rule on earth—still, time moves uniformly and indifferently along its inexorable course. In the bloody war year of 1863 Christmas was drawing near, with its tidings of love and joy.

I first heard of the coming of Christmas on a rainy October day —I was at that time a towheaded little fellow of four, the pampered youngest child of the family. I was watching the passageway with curiosity as hams, sausages and bacon, woolen stockings, shirts and underclothes and-most welcome of all— enormous rolls of tobacco were being carefully sewn into packages and labeled. For Christmas for your brothers in the war! was the answer to my question about the destination of all these fine things. For Christmas! These words were enough to awaken in my little head the slumbering memory of the splendors of the past Christmas. From now on I did nothing but pester my mother to tell me about Santa Claus and Christmas; and Little Red Riding Hood and Tom Thumb had lost all their attraction for me. My two sisters, who were then nine and eleven, exploited this opportunity for educational purposes, by threatening their little brother, on occasions when he was misbehaving too much even for the youngest of the family, that he would be completely ignored by Santa Claus; or, when he was good, whispering to him about the wonderful things that Santa

Claus carries in his sack for well-behaved children. Nor were their efforts entirely in vain, for I still remember how at this time I dedicated myself with great zeal and much success to my chores, which, to be sure, consisting merely of hunting for pins and nails, as well as pulling nails out of all old shingles and boards. Even Sally, the old black woman whom my father had bought less for the work she could perform than out of pity, stopped terrifying us with stories about witches and instead told us about the splendors of Kismus week, during which the slaves on most plantations were completely at liberty and all week long were allowed to live as if in a veritable fool's paradise. Father and Mother, to be sure, looked forward to Christmas with apprehension and were racking their brains about how to manage, in such troubled times, not to deprive the children of the eagerly awaited Christmas celebration. Often my mother would stay up until long after midnight, ripping up old clothes in order to turn them into new ones.

During the week before the celebration all kinds of strange experiments were carried out in the kitchen; since I could not very well be banished from the kitchen because of the prevailing wet weather, I was allowed to watch most of them. The problem was how to bake cookies for the Christmas tree without wheat flour, without raisins and almonds and all of the usual ingredients. And indeed the baking was successfully accomplished with finely ground corn meal and honey; instead of almonds and raisins, scalded peach kernels and shelled pecans were used for decoration. To us the cookies tasted splendid, but they had the disadvantage of being very brittle, and these little stars and animal figures soon fell from the tree. Concerning the candles for the tree, however, we were better off than we are today, for they were carefully molded of beeswax, and although they were not beautifully colored, like those we have now, they were all the more fragrant.

The day before Christmas brought a serious disturbance of our anticipation. Before daybreak my father was aroused from his sleep by the barking of dogs and anxious hallos. A boy brought him a message of such a serious nature that he rode off even before sunrise on his big trotting horse to Camp Groce near Hempstead. My recollection is that it had something to do with getting a fellow countryman out of trouble—a man who had been captured by the conscriptors and was to be courtmartialed. I don't know this for sure, and I can no longer find out anything about it, for of all those who were at my parents' house at the time, only old Sally is still alive, and she lost her memory years ago.

That evening my mother said, "If Father isn't back by tomorrow evening, then Santa Claus won't be coming either."—a terrible piece of news for us children.

The following morning rain was pouring down, and the dual concern about the arrival of my father and of Santa Claus increased from hour to hour. Whenever the rain stopped for a few minutes, I was certain to be found sitting on the tall gatepost keeping watch. Towards noon a norther came sweeping in, and the rain turned into sleet and snow; now I could stay at my post, where, to be sure, it soon became uncomfortably cool. It was probably three or four o'clock in the afternoon when my father finally came trotting along, thoroughly frozen but in an extremely good mood, so his mission must have been successful. In his saddle bags he brought along a precious treasure, four pounds of real genuine coffee, which he had been able to buy in Hempstead for two shiny silver dollars a pound. These saddle bags also concealed something else, which we children were not permitted to see. Now everything was fine again, and two ragged, miserable-looking soldiers on leave, who shortly afterwards asked for something to eat, probably had not had such a hearty welcome for a long time, or been shown such sumptuous hospitality.

Hardly had dusk arrived when the supper bell rang. I don't have much to report about the evening meal, since of course I was so excited that I couldn't get a bite down. This much I still recall, that on that evening, in honor of the event, instead of the usual prairie tea, coffee was drunk—not acorn, grain, or sweet-potato coffee, but coffee made from genuine freshly roasted beans that had just been shipped in. The main attraction of the meal, however, was an enormous wild tom turkey, which our cousin had killed the day before from his bedroom window.

And now we still had to wait for a little while in the kitchen. Normally it was pleasant there by the flickering fire, the most beautiful place to listen to tales being told. But our impatience was too great for anything like that, and soon the three of us, my sisters and I, were standing on tiptoe at the planked door, trying hard to peek through the cracks, while old Sally, to no avail, warned us of the sin of improper curiosity. Finally, finally: the longed-for ringing of the bell from the main house! In the greatest hurry we dashed through the dark passageway; on the porch, which was slicked over with ice, all three of us lost our footing, and I hit my head against a post so hard that at any other time it would probably have produced a cry of pain. Alarmed by the enormous commotion, our parents quickly opened the door, helped us safely back onto our feet, and now we plunged breathlessly into the room. I for my part had eyes only for the Christmas tree for quite some time. It was a beautiful, slender young wild peach tree that reached to the ceiling. For decorations they had used red berries from the woods, the Christmas cookies that had been so laboriously produced, and nuts in little baskets of colored paper. There were also candy sticks on the tree, but they had been made of brown Louisiana sugar and were not much to look at, although they had a marvelous taste. But two gigantic golden-yellow oranges, which my father had brought back from his trip, were the most marvelous thing on the whole tree. All these splendors stood out all the more strikingly against the dark, shiny deep green of the wild peach tree in which the numerous candles were reflected. In the doorway to the room old Sally was standing, and by the windows Colonel Bouldin's slaves, staring goggle-eyed, their mouths wide open, at the tree and the German Christmas celebration.

After my father, mother, and sisters had sung a Christmas song, everyone set out to inspect his share of gifts. My presents were stacked on a footstool under the tree, and I still see everything before me as if it were happening today. A straw hat, carefully woven of palmetto leaves by Grandmother Buntzel and with a wonderful red lining, as well as a new smock (back then boys were often still running around in little dresses until the age of eight) made of brown velvet with red dots—probably originating from someone's best dress—received no attention, although I later enjoyed them all the more. But there were also real toys: a fence that could be taken apart and put together at will, which had been whittled from an old box with a pocket knife by black Henry—a big good-for-nothing, but the smartest of Bouldin's Negroes; and inside the enclosure there was a little sheep, which probably was left over from an old Noah's Ark, but which had been given a coat of real wool and decorated with a little ribbon around its neck. If my boys get as much pleasure from the beautiful toys that Baby Jesus will bring them as I did from the little sheep, then I shall be well content.

Of the presents to others I still remember that everybody got a new pair of shoes made by shoemaker Necker of leather tanned in Frelsburg. Out of consideration I had been spared any such gift—indeed even ten years later any kind of footwear was still an object of my profoundest scorn. My father found at his place a pair of leggings made of the indestructible cloth woven by our neighbor and a velvet nightcap; my sisters found earrings and new clothes. For the grownups, meanwhile, a punch had been prepared, about which I have nothing to report except that it made our cousin so jolly that he started dancing on his crutch and missed by a hair toppling over the tree that had been set up so carefully. When the wax candles had all gone out the room was almost dark, for the lard-oil lamps and tallow candles produced only poor light, even though the latter had been placed in silver candlesticks in honor of the event. The grownups sat down around the table and told stories of times past in order to banish as much as possible any memory of the troubled present;

and I fell asleep over my toys and lapsed blissfully into the golden sleep of childhood, waking up the next morning with the little sheep clutched firmly in my hand.

This is how Christmas was celebrated in my parents' house in the terrible year of 1863. I would not be without this memory for any price; if I should ever be tempted to deprive my children of some joy, this memory would be the most effective admonition to provide for them what my parents granted me, and what nothing else in life can replace — a happy childhood.

*Wochenblatt Kalender fuer 1894 / Beilage zu No. 11 des Bellville Wochenblatts / Jahrgang 3. December 1893) pp. 8-13. Published in the Journal of the German Texas Heritage Society, Volume XXX, No. 4, Winter 2008.*

# The German Settlers of Millheim Before The Civil War

## Adalbert Regenbrecht[44]

The earliest German immigrants in Texas located in what is now Austin County. Friedrich Ernst and Charles Fordtran settled in 1831 where Industry now is. The families of Marcus Amsler, Ludwig Anton Sigmund von Roeder and Robert J. and Louis Kleberg settled in 1834 where Cat Spring now is. The reports these families sent to their former homes caused others to follow. Some of the experiences of these pioneers are recounted in The Quarterly, I, 297-302; II, 170-73 and 227-32.

Millheim was an offshoot of the settlement at Cat Spring.

The present article was prepared in response to a request of The Editors. It is printed as written, for the author died (March 29, 1916) very soon after it had been completed. He was in his eighty-fifth year, and, perhaps, the last survivor in Austin County of *die Lateiner*, those cultured, genial spirits who found it much easier to cultivate music and song and literature than corn and cotton. *Ubi libertas, ibi patria.*

---

44  Regenbrecht, Adalbert, *The German Settlers of Millheim (Texas) Before the Civil War*, Southwestern Historical Quarterly, Volume 20, No. 1, July 1916, pp. 28 - 34.

After the year 1848 several thousand highly educated Germans emigrated from Germany for various reasons, but immigrated to the United States from love of freedom. Not all of them went to the Northern States, but quite a number went to Austin County and other parts of Texas. My father was a professor of jurisprudence and was elected rector magnificus of the University of Breslau. As a young man he volunteered in the war of 1813 to 1815 and was decorated for bravery in the battle of Kulm with the iron cross and a Russian order. He was wealthy. In the year 1848 I was seventeen years old and a schoolboy. Therefore, I did not participate in the revolution, but took a lively interest in it. Reading the constitutions of the free countries I preferred the constitution of the United States. After having studied jurisprudence for several years and after the deaths of my parents I emigrated in company with a Texan farmer, who had married a second cousin of mine and returned with his wife to his farm in Austin County. We went in a sailing vessel to New Orleans and arrived there in January, 1856. Thence we went in a steamboat to Galveston, thence in another steamboat to Houston, thence in an ambulance drawn by mules to the farm of said farmer. In April I moved to Millheim, where I boarded with E. G. Maetze[45] and later with Dr. H. Nagel. In January, 1857, I bought a farm in Millheim. In June, 1857, I made a trip on horseback with five farmers, who wanted to inspect their lands in the Miller and Fisher grant in Llano County. We had a hack for our baggage, because we camped at night and for dinner. We went through La Grange, Bastrop, Austin, Burnet County to Castell and Leiningen on the Llano River. There I separated from them, who went directly to their homes, and rode alone to Fredericksburg, San Antonio and New Braunfels, at which place the 4th of July was celebrated. There I listened to the songs of a singing society. Thence I went back to Millheim. I carried no arms, because there was no danger of an attack by In-

---

45 Ernst Gustav Maetze (1817-1891). According to the *Texas Historical State Archives* (https://tshaonline.org/handbook/online/articles/fma11. Accessed August 27, 2017), he taught in the school in Millheim, retiring in 1878 and was elected in 1888 to the Texas Senate. He was married to Marie Langhammer – granddaughter of Franz Langhammer mentioned on page 88. (*Miller Family Papers*).

dians then in that part of Western Texas. Catspring and Millheim are adjoining. The first German immigrants arrived in Catspring in 1834 and in Millheim at least ten years later. In 1856 the hardships of pioneer life had gone. In these settlements were blacksmiths, wheelwrights, carpenters, shoemakers, tailors, brickmasons, a cabinet maker, a. saddler, a tanner, and a tinner. The ordinary farm laborer received free board and fifty cents per day. The teamster received fifty or seventy-five cents per hundred pounds for freight to or from Houston. The farmers of Millheim lived in frame dwelling houses, but some of the pioneer settlers lived still in block houses. The farms of the pioneer settlers were located where water and wood was handy, even where the soil was poor. Those who came later settled in their neighborhood, but most on the East of the old settlement on the black lands South of Mill creek. The Bernard Prairie extending from the Brazos to the Colorado and from Catspring to Brazoria County was a ranch free for cattle and horses. Therefore, many settlers were cattle and horse raisers. Some raised sheep, but with no success on account of depredation by wolves. Corn bread, bacon, molasses and coffee, occasional fish and venison, were the principal food of the pioneers.

In 1856 the settlers had better vegetable gardens and orchards and more milk, butter and cheese. There were more stores. Most farmers had wells or cisterns. There was a singing society in Millheim. In 1856 the farmers of Millheim at Catspring formed the Agricultural Society of Austin County at Catspring, which still exists, in which the book farmers of Millheim and the practical farmers of Catspring exchanged their knowledge. In Millheim was one of the best elementary schools of Texas, conducted by E. G. Maetze for more than twenty-five years. Many of his pupils became prominent, for instance, Charles Nagel, Secretary of Commerce and Labor ; Wm. D. Cleveland, of Houston, and Hugo Becker, wholesale merchants, W. A. Trenckmann, editor of Das Wochenblatt and State representative, and Wm. Hagemann, internal revenue officer. All Germans of Millheim were Democrats, but, as the Democratic Party in the

Southern States was for slavery, many Germans did not join said party. In the first election in which I participated I voted against secession. Ninety-nine votes were cast against secession, eight for secession at the Millheim-Catspring box. Nearly every one voted. According to my opinion the State of Texas had no better right to secede on account of slavery than the State of Utah on account of polygamy, slavery and polygamy being wrong. Nevertheless, I admit that the slaveholders were a noble class of people. Physically perfectly unfit for military service and opposed to the war, I succeeded in avoiding the service except that, although exempt as justice of the peace, I was compelled to go to the camp of instruction near Houston. After some weeks I was discharged by a writ of habeas corpus. The perfectly blind son of my neighbor Constant was carried to the same camp and detained there until his father succeeded in liberating him. Many Union men of our neighborhood enlisted in the Confederate Army because they believed it to be their duty. After the war I was probably the first justice of the peace in Texas in whose court a freedman recovered the wages for his labor from his former master. After the war I was appointed director of public schools and assessor and collector of taxes and elected four times county commissioner. After the Democratic Party had declared that the freedmen be protected by law I joined the party. Six German settlers of the small settlement of Millheim were former students at German universities, namely: E. G. Maetze, Dr. Nagel, Lawyer E. Kloss, Referendarius F. Engelking, Meisterlin and myself. Besides them lived there quite a number of highly educated Germans, for instance, Lieutenant Constant, Professor P. A. Trenckmann, Wilms, E. Kleberg, Robert and Alex. Kloss.

E. G. Maetze was born at Glogau in the Province Silesia of the Kingdom of Prussia on the 12th day of September, 1817. His father was the secretary of a Prussian general. In consequence of the war the family became poor. His wife kept a private boarding house with such success that her son could be educated in the gymnasium of Glogau and later in the university of Breslau.

After graduation he was appointed rector of the town school of Bernstadt. In 1848 he was elected a representative to the Prussian National Assembly. He joined the democratic wing of the Assembly. The royal government usurped arbitrary power. Therefore, the Assembly resolved that no taxes should be paid to the government. The resolution was not executed, because the people were tired of the frequent political disturbances and wanted peace and the government was supported by the army. The representatives who voted for said resolution, were prosecuted. E. G. Maetze escaped to Texas. He went to New Ulm and worked for a farmer. Hunting a horse in the Bernard Prairie he met F. Engelking, who invited him, to become a tutor of his children. Maetze accepted the proposal and a short time afterwards he established the first school at Millheim with six pupils at forty dollars per pupil in the first year. He bought a piece of land, on which he built a dwelling and outhouses, so that his wife and his two children could come to Texas and have a home. The number of pupils grew from year to year, not only from the neighborhood but also from distant places. He taught school at Millheim more than twenty-five years. He was a great speaker. His voice was euphonic, his gestures dignified, his speech logical. He joined the Democratic Party, but was opposed to secession. As his party was for secession, he did not vote. He submitted to the will of the people and became a loyal Confederate citizen. His son enlisted in Sibley's Brigade. In 1856 he was elected county commissioner, later senator and later county school superintendent. The Senate elected him its president pro tempore. The Democratic Executive Committee engaged him to make speeches in Fayette County to influence the Germans to join the Democratic Party. He was successful. He died on the 12th day of October, 1891, at the age of seventy-four years one month, highly respected by everybody.

A. F. Trenckmann, the son of a farmer, was born in Wefendishen near Magdeburg in the Kingdom of Prussia on the 7th day of July, 1809. He attended an elementary school and later a normal school, in which he graduated. As his means were insufficient, he had to supplement them in private teaching. Afterwards he established a private school in Magdeburg which became so popular that five hundred pupils attended the school at the same time. He was so prominent that in 1848 he was appointed as a member of a delegation to go to the King of Prussia and ask for political reforms. A. F. Trenckmann was progressive, but opposed to uproar and rebellion. In 1844 began a movement against pietiszmus[46] among the Protestants and against ultramontanismus[47] among the Roman Catholics, trying to harmonize belief and science. The Protestant movement originated in Magdeburg, the home of A. F. Trenckmann; the Catholic movement in Breslau, where my father and some others formed the sect of the "Christian Catholics," eliminating popery. A. F. Trenckmann sympathized with the Protestant movement. After the reaction of the religious and political reforms was successful, he emigrated in 1853, first to Colorado County, but in 1858 he bought a farm and gin in Millheim. He voted against secession, but obeyed the laws of the de facto government of the Confederate States and did not object to the enlistment of two sons in the Confederate Army at the beginning of the war; one of them was killed in battle. He was a good speaker and popular. He died in 1883. W. A. Trenckmann, his youngest son, is still living. He represented Austin County in the legislature some years ago and is editor and proprietor of one of the best German newspapers of Texas since many years.

[In preparing to write this article, Mr. Regenbreeht asked Hon. Charles Nagel[48] for a sketch of his father, Dr. Herman Nagel. Before receiving it he died. It is, however, added below.]

Dr. Hermann Nagel. — Born in Prittzwalk, Mark Brandenburg, Germany; attended the usual schools, and afterwards the Uni-

---

46 Pietism – a particularly pious group within the Lutheran Church founded by Philipp Spener (1635-1705) which spread into Protestantism. The movement is still extant, particularly in Southern Germany, today.
47 Ultramontanism -a political movement within the clerics of the Catholic Church which supports the power of the Pope above kings and councils.
48 See: Nagel C. *A Boy's Civil War Story*. CreateSpace; 2017. (Available on amazon.com ISBN 978-1547069101).

versities of Jena, Wurzburg, and graduated in medicine at the University of Berlin. Married Friedricka Litzmann, a daughter of a Lutheran clergyman; practiced his profession for a brief period, but in 1847 he and his wife sailed for New Orleans, where they arrived after the usual journey of many weeks, to continue it to the interior of Texas. They settled in Colorado County, about twelve miles from Columbus, on the St. Bernardo. The first intention was to abandon the profession, and to devote himself to the small farm which he had acquired. Very soon, however, the demand for medical aid was such that he returned to the practice of medicine, which profession he followed throughout his life. About 1855 he moved to Millheim, in Austin County, and again acquired a small farm, which was cultivated in the manner then in vogue, without, however, surrendering the professional pursuit. Life under these conditions no doubt answered every expectation and hope that had been entertained, until the breaking out of the Civil War, when conditions were naturally rendered difficult by the fact that Dr. Nagel sided with the Union cause.

In spite of the admitted need of medical men, and in spite of the very universal consideration with which he was treated, he concluded, in November, 1863, that it was no longer safe for him to remain at home. Leaving his wife and two children, he took his older son Charles with him, determined to make his way to Mexico. After many weeks of doubt and difficulty, they succeeded in crossing the border; from there made their way to Monterey; then to Matamoras, and from there by sail ship to New York, from which point they came to St. Louis. Landing here with fourteen dollars left, Dr. Nagel again established himself in his profession, and in the course of a few years had a comfortable income from his practice. After one year his wife (the two remaining children having in the meantime died), joined him, she having also come by way of Mexico and New York.

In 1872 Dr. Nagel visited Berlin, for the first time after leaving his native country, and while his son heard lectures in law, he spent another year in hearing lectures in medicine at this great University. Returning in 1873 he again practiced his profession, until the time of his death, in 1889.

While he was a man of very strong convictions, he took practically no part in public affairs, beyond exercising his rights as a voter. Although he had suffered his share of misfortune during the Civil War, he never entertained the remotest grievance against the Southern people. It was his opinion that the South thought itself right; that it had made a good fight; that happily the Union had been preserved, and that the energy of all citizens of the United States should be bent towards cementing all forces for the maintenance of that Union hereafter. How sincere he was in this feeling can perhaps be best exemplified by the simple statement that he voted for Samuel J. Tilden, and afterwards for Grover Cleveland, for President of the United States.

Charles Nagel read the article about Millheim settlers by Regenbrecht, and wrote this letter to the editor of the Southwestern Historical Quarterly; it appeared in Vol. 20, p. 413:

E. G. Maetze.—In a letter to the Editor, Mr. Charles Nagel pays the following tribute to E. G. Maetze:

"I read with particular interest the account of E. G. Maetze, whose country school referred to in the article, I attended. Only later in life did I learn to appreciate that probably Maetze was the ablest teacher I had ever had, and I say this, fully appreciating that rare fortune at one time or another had brought me into the presence of very competent men. As I recall it, Maetze must have been a born teacher. Books he had but few. However, he managed to present the accumulation of his own work to his pupils in such fashion that his pictures never faded. Today the impressions of Greek history that I treasured, go right back to the little school room at Millheim, where I can almost see my teacher telling the story of Marathon.

"I was first made conscious of the power of this man in 1893, while visiting the Chicago Exposition. Among the statues exhibited there was one entitled 'The Messenger from Marathon'. It was a very spirited statue, a replica of which I now possess, and the original of which I saw in Berlin in 1914. As I stood before it I involuntarily said to myself, 'that is precisely the way in which my teacher described it, and this led to the reflection, and finally to the conclusion that among all the teachers to whom it had been my privilege to listen, not one possessed his power to impress and to give out what he himself had attained."

# The Schoolmasters of New Rostock

## Texas Folk Play in Two Acts by William A. Trenckmann

Cast:
**Burkhardt**, teacher in New Rostock. Around 60.
**Carl Walther**, a young teacher.
**Wüster**, wealthy farmer and stockraiser.
**Wurm**, store and dance hall owner.
**Wenzel Baldrian**, a wealthy German-Bohemian.
**Brause**, county commissioner.
**Franz Freese**, Burkhardt's servant.
**Pat Muckleroy**, Irish mail rider.
**Gertrud**, Burkhardt's 18-year-old daughter.
**Adelgunde**, Wüster's wife.
**Elisabeth Alice**, Wüster's daughter.
**Aribert Johnnie**, Wüster's son.
**Marcus Junius Brutus Johnson**, a Negro boy.
Card players and musicians.

The play takes place in New Rostock, a German settlement in Texas that is not on the map; the time is 12 to 15 years ago. [As this was written in 1903, the approximate story time is 1887-1891].

## First Act

### First Scene.

Parlor at Wuster's house, tastelessly furnished.

Adelgunde and later Wüster.

**Adelgunde** (a somewhat elderly excessively thin lady in a black silk dress sits, reading a novel, in a rocking chair. A large coffee pot and an empty coffee cup are beside her on the table. Puts the novel aside and yawns). "Continued" again, and I will have to wait for two whole weeks before I know whether the count will find the treasure in the crypt and free the charming shepherdess.

And Wüster is still not here, and when he arrives he'll be drunk again for sure. Poor unfortunate woman that I am. I'll simply have to perish from impatience and unslaked thirst for revenge Finally, finally I can hope to revenge the insult Burkhardt paid me when he spurned me, the daughter of a royal Prussian colonist of stature, the wealthiest man In New Rostock, and a mother with noble lineage, for the sake of a desperately poor seamstress.

Our Aribert Johannes is the apple of Wüster'ss eye, and if our son's mistreatment by Burkhardt does not enrage my husband, then fish blood flows in his plebian veins. Indeed, my heart thirsts for revenge like that of the betrayed daughter of the pretzel baker, and revenge must be mine. Oh, If Wüster would only come home soon!

(Loud noise on the porch as if a saddle Is being dragged; Wüster, wearing boots and spurs and in an advanced state of inebriation, enters the door, trips over the doormat, and almost knocks over the coffee table while trying to catch himself.)

**Wüster.** This cursed doorrug.

The Schoolmasters of New Rostock 153

**Adelgunde** (jumping up). Disgusting, drunk again. Such vulgar behavior has to cause a woman of good family to despair. (Dries her eyes with her handkerchief.) O poor unfortunate woman that I am. Oh, my nerves!

**Wüster**. Never mind. Gundy, my sugar lump.

**Adelgunde**. Don't call me that! You know I hate that sort of vulgar nickname. It Is a fresh insult for me, poor down-trodden person that I am.

**Wüster**. Oh, fiddlesticks. Gundy. Well, I mean, don't be mad. After all, I traded the two lame old grays to a fool of a newcomer for a pair of good ponies and got fifty dollars to boot. I had to get the sucker drunk first and wound up a bit tipsy myself; that's just part of the business.

**Adelgunde** (praisingly). Oh, that's wonderful, dear hubby. Just give me the money so that I can lock it away till we send it to the bank. . . (Angrily.) Wüster, dear spouse, I must disclose something terrible to you. Our house has had unheard-of injury befall it.

**Küster**. What's the matter, did the expensive Poland China sow eat her piglets?

**Adelgunde**. Oh, something a thousand, a million times worse! Just think, the schoolmaster—the despicable vengeful man who cannot forget that I, at that time the greatest beauty far and wide, refused to listen to his pleas for love—has mistreated our poor Aribert savagely today, on the last day of school, has beaten him black and blue, so that the poor boy was not even able to sit at the lunch table until I salved his wounds with sweet
cream and gave him a cushion to sit on.

**Küster**. The devil you say! What did Johnny do this time?

**Adelgunde**. Oh, just imagine, a little piece of paper flew out of the poor sweet child's hand and stuck to the ceiling, and for this such an inhuman punishment with a cudgel as thick as your arm.

**Küster**. Ha ha ha, ho ho ho! He threw spitballs, the brat, that's what's the matter with Hannah. Just like his Dad! We always did that when I was a kid out West, and when the teacher once caught us and wanted to whip us, then Bill, the tall one, tripped him and we boys licked him so that he resigned and skipped out. Ho ho ho!

**Adelgunde** (aside). Frightful, this vulgar gibberish! (Aloud.) Oh Wüster, dear spouse, how can you laugh when our poor dear Aribert Johannes, your own flesh and blood, has been tortured. Oh, if you had heard how bitterly our dearest boy cried! Wüster, if you allow this insult to remain unavenged, then never appear before my eyes again.

**Küster**. You're right, Gundy; and I still have a score to settle with the old man because he spoiled my deal with tailor Schulze. I'll break his neck, damn him!

**Adelgunde**. Oh dear hubby, my little Wüster, you know you don't dare do that. But I, your spouse, will show you the way to get revenge. Burkhardt must lose his position; that will wound him more deeply than anything else you could do to him. Go and discuss the matter with Wurm; he hates him, too, and is much more clever than you are.

**Küster**. Well, you're not very complimentary, but I'll do it to please you. I'll ride to the store right away, and the schoolmaster will get his just desserts. So long. Gundy. (Leaves.)

**Adelgunde**. Frightful, this rotgut smell - and a lady of my high station has to endure this sort of thing!

### Second Scene.

Front room in Wurm's store.

Wurm, Freese, Baldrian, and Pat.

# The Schoolmasters of New Rostock

(To the left, in back, a bar with glasses; bottles on the shelves on the wall. To the right, in back, stairs leading to the dance floor upstairs. Further to the front on the side a window. To the right, toward the front, a card table at which Wurm and Pat Muckleroy, Freese and Wenzel Baldrian as partners are playing euchre. Wüster enters and kibitzes.)

**Kura** (taking the last trick). Hey, I've got the right bower (jack of trumps), you've been euchred and have to fork over. (Erases the chalk tab.)

**Freese**. Stop. You cheated. I saw clearly how Wurm pulled the right bower out of the deck.

**Kura**. Oh nonsense.

**Pat**. It's lying he is, the Dutch rascal.

**Baldrian** (tipsy, gets up and throws the cards down). You cheated and you're a wretched scoundrel. You seem to think Freese and the dumb Bohunk Wenzel are stupid people who can't notice when they are cheated by German and Irish rascals. I'll pay my bill this way (throws cards and glass on the floor. In parting.) I'll come back when the innkeeper is an honest man, catrocinnil – God keep you well.

(**Baldrian**, Freese, and Pat leave.)

**Küster**. Well, did they catch you this time, you crazy old humbug? You're usually as slick as an eel.

**Wurm**. I thought the jerks were too drunk to pay attention. The old dummy Pat is to blame; If it hadn't been for him, Freese wouldn't have noticed a thing.

**Wüster**. Well, never mind, we know each other. Say, Wurm, you don't like our schoolmaster.

**Wurm**. Why, what do you mean?

**Wüster.** Because he saw to it that you didn't pocket old lady Husemann's pension.

**Wurm.** Damn! Shut up!

**Wüster.** Never mind! No one is listening, and we two have known each other for a long time. And he managed to get the post office taken away from Mister Wurm too, because too many letters with "spondulicks" (money?) in them weren't delivered, you know. And he got Mister Brause made commissioner instead of Mister Wurm.

**Wurm.** Yes, if you already know, I hate the old sneak who turns the farmers against me.

**Wüster.** And takes the fattest cases away from you by getting the people to compromise.

**Wurm.** Yes, and he writes the deeds for them for free, and I can only lick my chops. Oh, I'll settle his hash (spit in his soup) so that he'll keep Wurm in mind.

**Wüster.** You're my man, Wurm, and I'll give you fifty dollars if we can get him out of the school. That's why I've come.

**Wurm.** Well, Wüster, I can't believe the part about the fifty dollars, you're too tight for that, but let me think. — I have an idea. Yes, by God, that's how we can do it! Open your ears and shut your mouth. (Whispering.) Saturday in four weeks is the election of trustees and the teacher. We'll both become trustees, and we'll elect another teacher.

**Wüster.** That won't work. The old hoosiers here will stick with Burkhardt, and where are you going to get another teacher?

**Wurm.** I'll do it. We'll put an ad for a teacher in a newspaper that no one around here reads. Then my nephew, Carl Walther, will apply. He's a very capable young man and has a normal school certificate. Besides the post-master, Commissioner Brause, and Doctor Rohrbach, only half a dozen people will come to the election.

**Wüster.** And they'll all vote for Burkhardt.

**Wurm.** Don't always interrupt with your jabbering when an intelligent person is speaking. The two Polacks on the Johnson's place I've got in my hip pocket, they've got to do what I want; we'll have the doctor called to the bedside of a severely 111 person in the river bottom, and I'll get Baldrian In line.

**Wüster.** You've spoiled things with him today with your cheating.

**Wurm.** Just let me handle it. The old sot can't stay away from my cider, and if I add a swallow from the big bottle to it and remind him that Burkhardt once said he wasn't bright enough to speculate in futures, then he'll vote the way we want. The stupidest guys. If they have money, cannot bear it if people don't call them clever. And tailor Schulze will also vote for my nephew if he can save four bits in school fees.

**Wüster.** Bully for you, Wurm. You're smart and should have become a real lawyer or a congressman. Ah yes, if someone has a fine education. And now lets take a drink.

**Wurm.** Not today, or you'll spill the beans at home - women can't keep their mouth shut. Go home now and tell your old lady not to scold you too much. And now get going toward home.

**Wüster** (Leaves. In the doorway, aside). A smart guy, Wurm, but only the devil can trust him. (Aloud.) Good bye, Wurm.

**Wurm.** Good bye. (Aside.) Repulsive fellow, but you can use that sort when you have to pull off the kinds of deals I do.

### Third Scene

Four weeks later.

Cozy parlor in Burkhardt's house.

Gertrud. Later her father and Brutus, a Negro boy who speaks Low German.

**Gertrud** (sitting at a table on which there is a basket with darned stockings and a bread and butter sandwich on a plate. Puts aside a book she's been reading, gets up, and sings as she rolls up the stockings—to the tune "Bald gras ich am Neckar, bald gras' ich am Rhein"):

I read about love and cannot understand

How I could lose my appetite because of heartache.

How I could kiss a total stranger—

If it were my father, that would be all right.

My heart should break if someone rejected it.

But it isn't a matchstick—that would be silly.

The poets are just fooling, there's no other way.

Else those in love would belong in the insane asylum. (Bites into the nearby sandwich)—Will I ever fall in love? You get warm and cold flashes when you read such beautiful poems about the joyful pain that you would sort of like to experience it, but if I would lose my appetite for a good sandwich, then I can do without it. . . Daddy should be returning home from the school meeting soon.

**Burkhardt** (with beekeeper's hood and equipment, enters, has the left hand tied up In his handkerchief). So, my little daughter, I got to the errant swarm in time. Caught it in the lower corner of the pasture before it could get into the brush. It's a big, beautiful swarm.

**Gertrud**. And my daddy is happy about that, but he's all worn out from the long hunt. Couldn't I have taken care of that for you, or old Franz?

**Burkhardt**. So that the bees sting your hands or even your red cheeks like they stung me. And our old Franz with his lame leg wouldn't have caught up with them by New Year's.

**Gertrud**. What, you've been stung as well. I'll put some tincture of hartshorn on it. (Does so.) So, is it all better now?

**Burkhardt**. It doesn't hurt a bit any more, and you know that Dr. Rohrbach said recently that bee stings were good against rheumatism. That's cheap medicine.

**Gertrud**. But Father, you seem to have forgotten that there is a school meeting today.

**Burkhardt**. I didn't forget, child, but I decided not to go again unless I was called. I'm of the opinion that it is more fitting for those people to remain amongst themselves. The teacher shouldn't help elect his own bosses.

**Gertrud**. But they are electing the teacher, too.

**Burkhardt**. Well, that's just a formal matter. I've been active here for almost a quarter of a century, have always done my duty with a good conscience, and now I need not fear anything.

(Someone knocks.)

**Burkhardt.** Come in!
   (Marcus Junius Brutus enters, but remains hesitantly in the doorway.)

**Burkhardt**. "Et tu Brute!" Well, what do you want? I'll bet you want one of Miss Gertrud's coffee cakes. Give him one, daughter.

**Brutus** (putting the small cakes offered him quickly into his pocket). Professor, here is a letter from Mister Wüster, and I have to go home right away, I don't have any time. (Runs away.)

**Burkhardt**. A cute scamp, that black Brutus. — A letter from Wüster, what might the meaning of that be? (Opens it and reads —starts again at the beginning.) Have I gone blind? That can't be possible—and yet, oh shameful!—by God I don't deserve that.

**Gertrud** (anxiously). What is it. Daddy? Let me read It. Not some misfortune?

**Burkhardt.** A misfortune for you perhaps, my child, but for me it is more, it's a base and undeserved slur on my honor of the sort that only a thoroughly worthless man could inflict on his worst enemy. In this letter—in Wurm's most beautiful handwriting—the teacher in New Rostock is informed that one has the honor of conveying the information to him that the school district of New Rostock—due to the increasing frailty caused by age of the present teacher—has elected Mr. Carl Walther, with six votes to three, to serve the next year as teacher, and that the teacher Burkhardt is requested to remove any of his possessions from the school house that may be there. Signed by Wüster, Wurm, and Baldrian as trustees.

**Gertrud.** Oh, I suspected that Wurm and Wüster, with whose villainous speculations you have Interfered, would get revenge.

**Burkhardt.** Indeed, they have gotten revenge—like villains. They've succeeded. The blow strikes home. That is the thanks for twenty years of faithful service in my office, for my having taught the children of our neighbors for next to nothing in times when these neighbors struggled on foreign soil for their existence, for my having not only striven to teach their children to read and write but to educate them to become moral and upright human beings, and for my having built the school house, from which I am being driven out like a criminal, almost entirely with my own hands. It is true that I've gotten old, I may no longer be modern in my pedagogical techniques, but to be chased away like a lame donkey whom one doesn't want to feed in his old age, that I do not deserve.

**Gertrud** (embracing her father). Father, dearest Father, don't take it so to heart. Every perceptive and right-thinking man from near and far esteems you highly; everyone knows that you have done more for New Rostock than could ever be repaid you with money. All of your former students love you like their father...

**Burkhardt**. And they stayed home when they should have done their duty at the school meeting and watched over the school to which they now send their children. They left the arena to these people.

**Gertrud**. Because none of them could even begin to suspect such a sneaky plot against you, no one would have thought it possible, and its execution will fill them all with horror and anger. — And Daddy, do you know what, your selfish daughter Gertrud is somewhat happy that things have happened this way, for now she will have her dear father all to herself, will be able to take care of him better and learn even more from him. My daddy won't have to go out to the school In rain or sleet, won't have to be aggravated by naughty children or slow learners and parents who don't understand their duties.

**Burkhardt**. And he'll sit at home, an old, useless man, who fiddles around a bit with his beehives and fruit trees and is a burden to his child.

**Gertrud**. A burden! — Daddy, you shouldn't speak that way, that hurts. You know that you are and will continue to be my only support, that I know no greater joy than to pamper you a bit, you who have been both a father and a mother to me for so long, and to serve you.

**Burkhardt**. Dear child, you mean well, and I thank you for that, but this blow not only hits me, old man that I am, but also you. You know that I am not wealthy.

**Gertrud**. You are richer than millionaires in love and good deeds.

**Burkhardt**. But from that my daughter will not be able to live when the time comes, and thus I regret the loss of my position doubly. To be sure I have a home, but I have little money, for, as little as I need for myself .

**Gertrud**. All the more you have sacrificed for the needy and for the common good.

**Burkhardt.** I certainly hope to be able to give you over to the protection of a man worthy of my daughter someday.

**Gertrud.** Father, I will never leave you.

**Burkhardt.** And when someday the right one comes, then you will go with him, for that is a woman's duty.

**Gertrud.** If one comes and he is really the right one, then he will not separate me from you but will help, in union with me, make your old age a sunny one.

**Burkhardt.** Child, in the face of your consolation, the outpourings of your filial love, all the shadows disappear, my courage reawakens, and I feel that I cannot let myself be bowed by an undeserved slight. When I came here I had become dispirited, though I was to be sure not so old as now, by a series of heavy blows of fate. In the love of you unforgettable mother and in my sphere of action I found courage and strength again. The death of your mother was the worst thing that has ever occurred to me, but you faithful filial love and my profession allowed me to recover my happiness, taught me to laugh. Being removed from my office hurts, but my dearest daughter will help me get over that too. And now come, let us go out into the arbor that your mother planted and marvel at the sunset.

**Gertrud** (clinging to her father). And chat about my mommy.

## Second Act.

### First Scene.

Evening of the annual masquerade ball in New Rostock. Parlor at the Wüsters' house. Family Wüster.

**Aribert Johnnie** (looking cautiously into the room and then entering). The old folks are still In the dining room and are eating

—and now's my chance—I'll get even with them for sure! They don't want to take me to the masquerade ball, for punishment, because I tripped the new professor with a wire over the school trail—just like the old man did to his teachers. And the paddling was good for Johnnie, and when old Burkhardt paddled me about half as hard they made a fuss and kicked him out of the school. (Has in the meantime taken the book-marker out of the installment of the novel his mother had been reading, smeared the lenses of her glasses with tallow, and poured ink from a pen on her handkerchief that lies next to the glasses.) And now for the old man. (Extracts a darning needle from his mother's sewing basket and puts it in his father's upholstered easy chair.) Won't he jump? And Sister Liza put her two bits worth in, saying I shouldn't go; I'll settle with her. (Takes a large square piece of paper and writes on it in large letters.)

>
> **FLOUR KVEEN**
>
> **LIZA**
>
> **WUESTER**

Well, she'll be fighting mad when everyone recognizes her. And now I've got to skip, the old lady's coming. (Leaves.)

**Adelgunde.** Now I can continue to read my novel before Elisabeth finishes with her costume, and by the time she and Wüster return I may have finished it. (Picks up the installment, leafs through it, puts on her glasses.) What's the matter with my glasses, I can't see anything. (Johnny looks through the door, which is slightly ajar, or through the window with visible signs of great glee.) I'll have to wipe off my glasses. (Does so and gets her hands black and, when she puts on the glasses, her face as well.) That cursed brat Johnny did this. Oh, that good-for-nothing. Wüster! Wüster! (Johnnie disappears.)

**Wüster** (rushing in). What's up! Did you see a mouse, or are you getting hysterics again?

**Adelgunde.** Just look what your Johnnie, your dear son, has done, how he has made a laughing stock of me, his own mother. You must punish him immediately and teach him a lesson.

**Wüster** (beginning to laugh upon catching sight of his wife). Ho ho ho! Gee wlllikins, you're a sight. (Sits down, weak with laughter, in his easy chair, only to jump up with a scream of pain and a curse; he finds the darning needle and chases out with the cry): I'll break his confounded neck!

(Johnnie, who in the meantime has been dancing a war dance for joy at the window, disappears again.)

**Adelgunde** (who at first had giggled, hurries after her husband). Wüster, don't you dare mistreat my poor Aribert.

**Elisabeth Alice** (coming, dressed as a flower queen, but without a mask, from the next room). Oh, Mamma, I have something to tell you. — Why Mother, you look like a nigger!

**Adelgunde.** Speak German, my child. You know that I don't understand English and hate crude gibberish (German mixed with English).

**Elisabeth.** Mamma, I have a favor to ask. You know that I've set my cap for Professor Walther, the only stylish young man In the settlement, and though he hasn't proposed to me yet, I know he adores me.

**Adelgunde.** I know, my daughter, and I am thrilled, for as an educated mother it is my goal that my daughter gets an educated husband and not a rustic hick of a armer.

**Elisabeth.** Well, Mamma, then help me manage the old man; he wants me to marry a rich stock raiser or something like that.

**Adelgunde**. Stay calm, my child, you are my daughter, and Wüster will do what I want.

**Wüster** (enters, groaning and rubbing his nose). The damned scamp! Runs under the washline so that I almost tear my head off and fall against the pigpen and have to listen to him laugh. But I'll get him yet, and then I'll skin him alive.

**Adelgunde**. Dearest spouse, don't get so worked up about the pranks of a head-strong boy.

**Wüster**. Head-strong, indeed.

**Adelgunde**. We have something more important to discuss now. It's a question of the future and fortune in life of our Elisabeth. (Elisabeth caresses her father.) Elisabeth just made a stirring confession to me. She loves young Professor Walther, a highly educated man.

**Wüster**. And a poor wretch of a schoolteacher with whom she can suck on stripped pig's feet for hunger.

**Adelgunde** Don't always interrupt me; you know I can't stand that. Professor Walther is a highly trained gent, and his education could be of use to you.

**Wüster**. Well, there's something to that. That's no lie, but she can maybe get someone who has plenty of tin.

**Adelgunde.** Quiet, Wüster. I'm telling you that Elisabeth will marry the professor and that's that. You are my dear sensible hubby and I know you only want the happiness of your family.

**Wüster**. Well, that settles the hash. Perhaps we can turn the starveling of a schoolteacher into a merchant or a lawyer. Come, Alice, we have to get started.

**Elisabeth**. Dear old Daddy! Good-bye, Mamma. (While standing in the door.) Oh, Mamma, make Johnny go to bed now; he's still outside here by the buggy.

**Johnny** (entering). Good-bye, Liza. -- I fixed her up good.

**Second Scene.**

Parlor at Burkhardt's house. Burkhardt, Gertrud, and later Freese.

**Burkhardt** (sitting at his desk with a large account book lying before him, puts the book aside). My dear daughter still doesn't seem to be ready. Freese's been waiting for a long time. She is usually so quick to get dressed, more than most of Eve's sex.

**Gertrud** (very cute In her fisher girl costume, rushes into the parlor and stands suddenly in front of her father). Is this all right. Daddy?

**Burkhardt**. By golly yes, my dear. I'm quite sad that I can't come along to show you off. (Teasingly.) I really think you would be able to catch a very big fish in your net. Watch out, however, what kind of fish, for in ballrooms the rotten fish sometimes have the most attractive scales.

**Gertrud**. Don't tease, not tonight. Daddy. I'm really not in the mood for dancing and I'd prefer to stay with you so that you don't stay up till past midnight, like last night, working on the accounts of the treasurer who absconded.

**Burkhardt**. Well, child. I'd like to go along, but you know that I promised to go through the books by Monday so that when a new county treasurer is selected in place of Allen it is at least known how much Allen embezzled from the county. And with the confusion in the books that is no easy task. It's not a good thing for youth to separate itself from youth, and you shouldn't go sour here with your old father. Our young people may not be as carefully dressed according to the fashion journal as the townspeople, and they are a bit stiff in the ballroom, but they are upright and decent young men. You are not lowering yourself to dance with them, and besides I know that my daughter is so well bred and of such a nature that no one will try anything untoward with her. On the way there our old Franz will protect you like the apple of his eye.

**Gertrud**. It will be hard to enter the establishment of the man who behaved so badly toward you.

**Burkhardt**. Wurm runs a public establishment, and besides it has been rented for this evening by the school district for the masquerade ball.

**Gertrud**. But Father—it may sound foolish—I am most reluctant to meet your successor, the present teacher. I don't know why, but every time I see him I get cold chills and hot flashes; I'm almost afraid I hate him.

**Burkhardt**. That sounds dangerous. A reader of novels might read something in your statements you haven't thought of. But seriously, my dear girl need not draw back from anyone and—one should always give people their just due—according to everything I have learned indirectly, I believe that young Walther is an upstanding young man, in any case a capable and conscientious teacher who keeps his pupils in order better than old Burkhardt did In his day, and now go, dear child, and have fun.

**Freese** (calling from outside). Miss Gertrud, the horses don't want to wait any longer, and I hear the fiddles and accordion already.

**Gertrud** (kissing her father). Good night, dear Father; I'll come back soon.

**Burkhardt**. Don't come back too early; stay as long as you're having fun. Good night. Take care of our child, Franz.—The sweet girl.—May God help her find the rich good fortune that she deserves. (Takes up a pen.) So the old German schoolmaster, since he learned arithmetic, can be useful for something when it's a matter of summing up a lost life. Poor Allen—he was a nice, friendly man whom everyone had to like and now he is an absconded thief, and a spendthrift foolish follower of fashion is to blame who didn't understand how to offer her husband a home but rather brought about his financial ruin, drove him to gambling and finally to embezzlement, because he lacked a firm character.

### Third Scene.

Front room in Wurm's establishment.

(Wurm is busy behind the bar, on which many empty bottles are standing as well as a few full ones, and also a big tub of lemonade. To the left stands the card table, at which Wüster, Pat, and two rather shabby characters are playing solo. Freese is sitting to the right, along the wall toward the front. During the game Walther, disguised as a hunter but without a mask, comes down the steps and positions himself by the window.)

**Walther** (aside). The tobacco smoke isn't much better than the dust upstairs. But at least I've given the horrible flower queen, on whom a bad boy hung that ridiculous sign, the slip, covered by people promenading — I could see how she was aiming my way for the ladies' choice after we took off our masks. If I were gallant I should have called her attention to the trick some boy played on her but I just can't stand her and my mom always says, "He who puts himself in danger suffers the consequences." Now if it had been the sweet fisher girl, that would have been a different matter. I was able to dance with her twice, but now that the masks are off that's probably a thing of the past.

**Wurm** (aside). So, now I'm running out of cider, and Wüster alone is good for another half dozen bottles, for tonight he's getting blind drunk. (Dips water out of a bucket into a couple of half-emptied bottles.) That'll do the job just as well, the guys can't taste it any more anyway, and I can for once serve holy Temperance.

(In the meantime the game has run its course. Cries such as "Here's a marriage!" "The ace of spades goes along face down!" "Diamond solo!" "I'm playing null ouvert!" "Rum is not

Kümelschnapps!" From upstairs a shuffling can sometimes be heard as if from dancers, also individual notes from an accordion.)

**Wüster** (after looking at his cards). Club solo. Here is the queen of clubs, the seven of clubs, the queen of spades, the ace of clubs; so, then four diamonds. You've been skunked, you sots! Hurrah for we, us, and company. Well, don't look so sad, you suckers, today Wüster is setting up. Bring on the cider, Wurm, or give the guys a slug from the bottle the revenue man doesn't know about.

**Pat**. Hurrrah for Mister Wooster! Give me a drop of creature comfort. (They drink.)

**Wüster**. Fill'em up again. Give them snake poison again, Wurm, the loafers. Do you know why? Because my Alice is going to marry the schoolmaster.

**Wurm** (warningly, since he just notices Walther). Shut your trap, camel! Walther is down here.

**Wüster**. That's all hunky dory. Come here, son-in-law! (Getting up and offering him a glass.) Here, son-in-law, slug one down with us. You may have my Alice, even if you are a hungry sucker with only bread to eat.

**Walther**. Excuse me. Mister Wüster, but you've made a mistake.

**Wüster**. Mistake, oh stuff. Don't play dumb like that. I've told you that you may have my Alice, and she gets ten thousand blank ones and a farm and fifty head of Herefords to boot. My old lady wants it that way.

**Walther** But I have no intention of wooing for your daughter's hand, and Miss Alice has no thought of wanting me as her husband.

**Wüster**. Whaaat! You don't want to, you damned fool! You— don't want to; by God. I'll knock you down. (Goes up to him with upraised fist.)

**Walther.** (looking him firmly in the eye). Don't dare! I do not wish get into a knock-down drag-out fight with a drunken man, but if it must be, I can defend myself.

**Pat.** Go to It, Wooster, give it to him, begorra!

**Wüster** (first steps back, then draws a bowie knife and, swaying to and fro, approaches Walther). Damn you. I'll kill you. (Freese has in the meantime jumped up and knocks the knife out of Wüster's hand with his heavy walking cane. Wüster, when Walther approaches him, runs away through the side door cursing, crying out): I'll get you yet!

**Pat.** Hip, hip, hurrah for the schoolteacher! You're my man. Set 'em up, professor.

**Walther.** Not tonight, Pat. Freese, I thank you for saving me from the attack of this man or from having to knock him down. (Shakes his hand.)

**Freese.** It's nothing, I enjoyed it myself that I could hit the dirty pig on his trotters. And now I want to hitch up the horses again, for Miss Gertrud wants to go home soon. (Exits, with him Pat and the other card players.)

**Wurm.** Listen, Nephew, what kind of stupid things are you doing? You've insulted the richest man in New Rostock, who's also your boss, and are throwing over the rich girl. She's a bit dumb, to be sure, but that does no harm, and ten thousand dollars are no trifle.

**Walther.** Uncle, It's difficult for me to answer you, for you are my dear mother's brother and I owe my position to you. Nevertheless, it must be said: your ways are not my ways. I am not a scoundrel who sells himself for money. You committed a grievous injustice in concert with that crude Wüster when the two of you removed my predecessor from office through deceit.

**Wurm.** Don't be a fool.

**Walther.** You may consider me a fool — I don't want to have anything in common with cheaters and scandalmongers and tomorrow I am going to resign from the position I did not attain through legitimate means. Good-bye, Uncle. I want to catch some fresh air.

**Elisabeth** (rushes, without a mask, down the stairs with the "Flour Kveen" sign in her hand). Oh, Papa, Papa, take me home. I've been insulted. The schoolteacher insulted me; he stuck this paper on my back.

**Wurm.** Miss Alice, your dear father is outside enjoying the moonlight (moonshine?). (Elisabeth hurries out the door.)

**Wurm.** The stupid goose. What a mistake to think my nephew would choose something like that. — A complete ass, my nephew, or — as others would say — a German man of honor: it's all the same. Let him go. But it occurs to me that ten thousand dollars and a farm and fifty head of Herefords and all that goes with those things would be something for the son of my father. If cotton goes up for another three days on the exchange I'm bankrupt. Perhaps Wüster's little goose will take the uncle if she can't get the nephew. Better to have a dumb wife than nothing to gobble down. I'll strike the iron while it's hot.

(Twirls his mustache and goes outside.)

**Walther** (entering). I'd like best to go home after this wild scene, but it would appear cowardly and I'd like to see the fisher girl once more — perhaps for the last time.

**Gertrud** (calling out from above). Freese! Freese! (Enters.) He's not here either. (Notices Walther and steps back.)

**Walther** (aside). That's the way it is, she despises me and I can't blame her. (Aloud.) Miss Burkhardt, Mr. Freese is outside hitching up. Should I call him?

**Gertrud.** Oh no, thank you. I'll go to him, for we're going home now.

**Walther**. Miss Burkhardt, I know that you cannot esteem me. Tomorrow I am departing from here forever, and I wouldn't like for you to remember me as a man who, in concert with Wüster and my uncle (I'm ashamed to have to call him that), drove your father, whom I must esteem as a teacher and as a man, from his position, stole it from him. I implore you, grant me a word.

**Gertrud** (aside). He wants to leave here. How gladly I believe that he is not at fault. (After a brief hesitation.) Mr. Walther, I am ready to hear what you have to say to me.

**Walther**. I thank you and ask you for yet another proof of your confidence. May I accompany you to Freese?

**Gertrud**. I will follow you. (He offers her his arm and the two leave the front room.)

**Wurm** (rushing in). Well, I really messed up on that one. This goose of a woman—she called me a hunch-backed cross-eyed camel, this—this amiable lady. Well, I'm no real beauty, but I'm not as dumb as the Wüster family, here's nothing doing there. Well, a small bankruptcy with a settlement at ten percent on the dollar is in the end not as bad as having such a fury as a wife. You can live with that a lot better. But a proper bankruptcy proceeding will cost money and the stockbrokers have squeezed me dry.

Voice from above cries out: Five lemonades, one soda water!

**Wurm**. My lemonade tub is empty, but Wurm knows how to help himself. (Empties both water buckets in the lemonade tub.) There are still some seeds in there, and Wurm can make good use of the six nickles now.

### Fourth Scene.

Early in the morning on the following day.

Burkhardt, Gertrud, Freese, Walther, Brause, Wenzel Baldrian, tailor Schulze, and the musicians. Burkhardt's parlor. Gertrud in a housedress with a white apron puts the feather duster aside. Goes to the window and stands there pensively.

**Gertrud** (sings. Mel.: "Ach wie ist's möglich dann"): Will that man come whom I have in my heart.
   Who forced me to love?
   I'm so fearful.
   Were he never to come.
   I'd not ever want to breath again;
   I'd still think of him in the coffin.

What sort of nonsense am I singing there? Who is supposed to come? — Walther? He wants to leave here today. Everything seems like a dream to me: first I hear the melodies of the dance music, then the sound of his voice in my ear. (Pensively.) — Did I really tell him that he could hope if he succeeded in gaining the respect and confidence of my father? I'm a real muttonhead. — And today is Daddy's birthday, and I've got to hurry to set the table before he returns from his morning stroll. Daddy doesn't want to see a dreamy, sad face.

(Puts a cake and a bunch of flowers on the table and lays a bathrobe and a velvet cap next to it. — Burkhardt enters; Gertrud flies to him and embraces him.)

**Gertrud.** Dear, dear Daddy, happy birthday! (Gives him a kiss.)

**Burkhardt.** By golly, girl, you've never hugged me as stormily as that, and your kiss — just as if I were your sweetheart and not an old graybeard of a father.

**Gertrud** (blushing and embarrassed). You are my sweetheart, Daddy. (Puts the bathrobe on him, puts on his cap for him, and leads him to the birthday table.) And now, Daddy, come to breakfast.

**Burkhardt.** Child, first you have to tell me about the masquerade ball. (There is a knock at the door.) Come in. (Franz enters with a large sealed letter.) Where did you get that enormous letter so early in the morning?

**Freese.** Well, the old sleepyhead Pat in his usual drunken state must have stuck it next to the mailbox, because I found it on the ground.

**Burkhardt.** I'm curious (opens the letter with a pen knife, reads a few lines) — come here, Gertrud, dear daughter, this letter you should read along with me.

(Gertrud reads the letter with her father, leaning up against him, begins a dance of joy through the parlor, then hugs and kisses her father again.)

**Gertrud.** Father, how happy this news makes me that will erase the memory of the ingratitude and injustice shown you from your memory. I knew that every upstanding man would have to recognize your services and that you will still do much good for your fellow man.

**Burkhardt.** This letter, bringing news of my appointment to a position of high confidence, makes me happy, too. I'd have to lie if I wanted to say that the words of recognition from the mouths of our upright county judge and the commissioners didn't please me. Age is no protection against the minor sin of vanity. But more than this it makes me happy that I — if God should allow me to live another few short years — will be able to take care of my Gertrud. But come to breakfast now, my little daughter, for a good meal is soothing for the nerves after such excitement. Come along, Freese. (They want to go.)

**Freese.** Hey, there's someone coming.

**Gertrud** (looks through the window: aside). Heavens, it's Walther. (Runs out the side door.)

(There is a knock.)

**Burkhardt** (aside). He's picked an inconvenient time to visit, I must say. (Aloud.) Come in. Well, where has Gertrud gone to? She's not usually a timid little goose.

**Walther** (enters and approaches Burkhardt). Mr. Burkhardt, please excuse me for coming to you so early. My name is Walther and I feel that I should have come much earlier.

**Burkhardt**. You are welcome today and at any time. After I was active as a teacher for so long it's natural that my interest in the school has not vanished with the cessation of my activities there, and it was a great pleasure to hear that my successor carries out his office with eagerness, conscientiousness, and good success.

**Walther**. I thank you for these words, which I could scarcely expect from a man who has been so grievously wronged. And yet they shame me deeply. As soon as I took up my position here I had to recognize that my predecessor had to have been not only an outstanding teacher, a model for his fellow teachers, but also a worthy man. For the past few days I have known that I myself came here in your place as teacher through a heinous conspiracy, and I can only surmise how deeply you must have been hurt by something for which my close blood relative deserves the primary blame. Since I learned this, the decision has solidified that I must make retribution for all that happened without my knowledge to the extent that I am able. My resignation is in the hands of the trustees.

**Burkhardt**. You shouldn't have done that. You have been appointed to this position, have exercised it loyally, and you must remain there. I, myself, will never be a teacher here again. But you could not have given old Burkhardt a greater joy than you just did with your manly declaration. (Clasps both his hands.) I'm proud of my young friend and successor Walther. And now sit down for a moment. I just want to call my daughter, who has just now run away from us. You must meet her, too, and then you must share our delayed breakfast with us. (Wants to go.)

**Walther**. Mr. Burkhardt, before I settle down as a guest in your house I must, as an honorable man, tell you more, something that may cost me your confidence that I just now gained. Mr. Burkhardt—I love your daughter; I ask you for permission to win Gertrud's love, to sue for her hand.

**Burkhardt**. Wha—t, you love my Gertrud, desire her as your wife. For heaven's sake, how did that happen? Certainly, If my daughter wants you. I'll give my blessing, for I rely on the voice of her pure heart. But I must first ask her myself. (Wants to go.)

**Gertrud** (entering slowly, throws herself on her father's breast). Father, I want to. I love him more than I can say.

**Burkhardt** (kisses her on the forehead). Then there is your place by God's commandment and that of your heart, now and forevermore. (Removes her arms from his neck, leads her to Walther, and places her hands in his.) Take her, my son, and prove yourself worthy of her. I give you in her my most precious, my only jewel, and I do so gladly. Be happy, my children.

(Walther and Gertrud stand silently in an ardent embrace. )

**Gertrud**. Good lord, my father is crying!

**Burkhardt**. They are tears of joy which hope and firm trust in the future cause to flow. May a pure joy blossom forth In you like that I enjoyed with your mother in these narrow rooms.

**Freese** (who had been standing in the open door for several minutes with signs of lively sympathetic interest, entering). No, something like this I've never seen all the days of my life, that folks moan and cry when they get engaged. — Congratulations, my dear Trudie and Herr Schoolmaster, and I want you to be sure to make the girl happy.

**Gertrud**. Thank you, good old Franz. But you have something wet in your eyes, too.

**Freese** (while Walther is shaking his hand with authority). Oh, stuff, how would an old fellow like me cry. I just have a dumb cold. (Wipes his eyes with a handkerchief with large flowers on it and limps hurriedly out.)

**Burkhardt**. And now children, come to breakfast. Young love may be enough food for you two but joy and emotion have got me to where I can hardly keep standing. — Daughter, see if the coffee hasn't gotten cold.

(Music by strings or brass on the porch: "Heil Dir im Siegerkranz" or a similar melody suitable for an accolade.)

**Everyone**. What's the meaning of that?

(A flourish, then there is a knock.)

**Burkhardt**. Come in.

(Brause, Baldrian, and tailor Schulze enter; musicians in front of the open door.)

**Burkhardt**. Welcome, dear neighbors. Sit down.

(Everyone remains standing.)

**Brause** (stepping forward). Schoolmaster, I've just come from the county seat with the splendid news that our old Burkhardt has been unanimously elected as county treasurer, because we couldn't have found a more upstanding and better man to guard our treasury. We all want to congratulate you and hope that you'll accept the office but won't completely forsake our settlement, since we can't do without Burkhardt here at home either.

**Burkhardt**. I will certainly accept the office and serve faithfully as you expect me to. And I will certainly not leave New Rostock, these four corner posts and the place where my wife lies buried, unless I have to.

**Everyone**. Hurrah. Cheers for our new treasurer Burkhardt.

**Baldrian** (steps forward). Your abashed servant. I beg your pardon. Wenzel Baldrian was a stupid scoundrel, let himself be misled by that dog Wurm, voted against old Burkhardt. Please forgive dumb old Wenzel Baldrian.

**Burkhardt** (shakes his hand). That's all right, Baldrian, I know you have your heart in the right place, but schnapps is your worst enemy.

**Tailor Schulze.** Honored Sir, I would like to address so to speak for the most part a few words to you since I so to speak became a common scoundrel along with Baldrian with respect to our professor so to speak. And I ask, don't hate me for it that I for the most part so to speak am just a bit too economical by nature and so to speak I have always esteemed you highly so to speak so to speak—for the most part. . . . Thunderation, now I have for the most part so to speak let my words get (gallop) away from me, so to speak.

**Burkhardt.** Well, no harm done. I certainly don't bear a grudge; and though it was indeed painful for me at the time, today it seems to me that it was a miraculous, benign stroke of fate that you set my chair before the door then. You all can, it seems to me, be quite content with the exchange of schoolmasters, and I am especially satisfied, for my successor, here my young friend Walther, will soon become my son-in-law.—But now pardon us, dear neighbors, we haven't had any breakfast with all this commotion, and that's nothing for an old man. The fire In the kitchen has probably gone out by now.—Freese—Where has Freese gotten to?

**Freese** (enters with a basket full of bottles of wine). I'm coming. I think we can use these.

**Burkhardt.** You're right, old man. All right, neighbors, take an early drink of wine from my own press and eat a piece of my birthday cake with it.

> (Walther and Freese in the meantime have begun to open bottles and to pour out wine, while Gertrud cuts the cake.)

**Brause** (starts the tune, whereupon the others join in). Long live our old schoolmaster. Three cheers.

**Everyone** (as above). Long live our young schoolmaster. Three cheers. Hurrah, hurrah, hurrah.

**Baldrian**. And his pretty fiance&e . as well.

**Everyone**. Hurrah, hurrah, hurrah.

(Flourish. The curtain falls.)

Printed in the *Bellville Wochenblatt*, Supplement, Vol. 13, December 24,1903 translated by Hubert P. Heinen. Published in the German-Texan Heritage Society Newsletter, Vol. VIII, No. 3, Fall 1986. Volume VIII Number 3 Fall.

# Life of German Pioneers in Early Texas.

## Caroline von Hinueber (Born Ernst)[49]

When my father came to Texas, I was a child of eleven or twelve years. My father's name was Friedrich Ernst. He was by profession a book-keeper, and emigrated from the duchy of Oldenburg. Shortly after landing in New York he fell in with Mr. Fordtran, a tanner and a countryman of his. A book by a Mr. Duhde, setting forth the advantages of the new State of Missouri, had come into their hands, and they determined to settle in that State. While in New Orleans, they heard that every settler who came to Texas with his family would receive a league and labor of land from the Mexican government. This information induced them to abandon their first intention.

We set sail for Texas in the schooner *Saltillo*, Captain Haskins. Just as we were ready to start, a flatboat with a party of Kentuckians and their dogs was hitched on to our vessel, the Kentuckians coming aboard and leaving their dogs behind on the flatboat. The poor animals met a grievous fate. Whenever the wind arose and the waves swept over the boat, they would howl and whine most piteously. One night the line parted, and we never saw them again.

We were almost as uncomfortable as the dogs. The boat was jammed with passengers and their luggage so that you could hardly find a place on the floor to lie down at night. I firmly be-

---

49  von Hinueber, Caroline Ernst, "Life of German Pioneers in Early Texas", Southwestern Historical Quarterly, Volume 2, January 1899, pp. 227 - 232.

lieve that a strong wind would have drowned us all. In the bayou, the schooner often grounded, and the men had to take the anchor on shore and pull her off. We landed at Harrisburg, which consisted at that time of about five or six log houses, on the 3d of April, 1831. Captain Harris had a sawmill, and there was a store or two, I believe. Here we remained five weeks, while Fordtran went ahead of us and entered a league, where now stands the town of Industry.

While on our way to our new home, we stayed in San Felipe for several days at Whiteside Tavern. The courthouse was about a mile out of town, and here R. M. Williamson, who was the alcalde, had his office. I saw him several times while I was here, and remember how I wondered at his crutch and wooden leg. S. F. Austin was in Mexico at the time, and Sam Williams, his private secretary, gave my father a title to land which he had originally picked out for himself. My father had to kiss the Bible and promise, as soon as the priest should arrive, to become a Catholic. People were married by the alcalde, also, on the promise that they would have themselves reunited on the arrival of the priest. But no one ever became Catholic, though the priest, Father Muldoon, arrived promptly. The people of San Felipe made him drunk and sent him back home.

My father was the first German to come to Texas with his family. Hertzner, a tailor, and Grossmeyer, a young German, at Matagorda, both unmarried, were in Texas when my father came. There was also a Pennsylvanian, whom they called Dutch Henry, and a Dr. Adolph v. Zornow, had traveled through Texas, but did not stay long. My father wrote a letter to a friend, a Mr. Schwarz, in Oldenburg, which was published in the local newspaper. This brought a number of Oldenburgers and Münsterländers, with their families, to Texas in 1834.[50]

50 [Robt. J. Kleberg, Sr., writes: "We had accidentally got hold of a letter written by a gentleman, who had emigrated some time before us from the Duchy of Oldenburg and who lived where now is Industry, Texas, Fritz Ernst, by name. In this letter he had described Texas, then a province of Mexico, in very glowing colors, mentioning also the advantages offered to immigrants by the Mexican government, namely, a league and labor for every man with a family and ½ league for every single man. This letter caused us to change our first intention to go to one of the northern states

After we had lived on Fordtran's place for six months, we moved into our own house. This was a miserable little hut, covered with straw and having six sides, which were made out of moss. The roof was by no means water-proof, and we often held an umbrella over our bed when it rained at night, while the cows came and ate the moss. Of course, we suffered a great deal in the winter. My father had tried to build a chimney and fireplace out of logs and clay, but we were afraid to light a fire because of the extreme combustibility of our dwelling. So we had to shiver. Our shoes gave out, and we had to go barefoot in winter, for we did not know how to make moccasins. Our supply of clothes was also insufficient, and we had no spinning wheel, nor did we know how to spin and weave like the Americans. It was twenty-eight miles to San Felipe, and, besides, we had no money. When we could buy things, my first calico dress cost 50 cents per yard. No one can imagine what a degree of want there was of the merest necessities of life, and it is difficult for me now to understand how we managed to live and get along under the circumstances. Yet we did so in some way. We were really better supplied than our neighbors with household and farm utensils, but they knew better how to help themselves. Sutherland[51] used his razor for cutting kindling, killing pigs, and cutting leather for moccasins. My mother was once called to a neighbor's house, five miles from us, because one of the little children was very sick. My mother slept on a deer skin, without a pillow, on the floor. In the morning, the lady of the house poured water over my mother's hands and told her to dry her face on her bonnet. At first we had very little to eat. We ate nothing but corn bread at first. Later, we began to raise cow

and to choose Texas for our future home. At the time we left, hardly anything was known of Texas, except that my ideas and those of my party were formed by the above mentioned letter, in which Texas was described as a beautiful country, with enchanting scenery and delightful climate, similar to that of Italy, the most fruitful soil and republican government, with unbounded personal and political liberty, free from so many disadvantages and evils of old countries. Prussia, our former home, smarted at the time we left under a military despotism. We were enthusiastic lovers of republican institutions, full of romantic notions, and believed to find in Texas, before all other countries, the blessed land of our hopes." This is taken from notes written by him in 1876. — R. K., Jr.]

51  See next paragraph.

peas, and afterwards my father made a fine vegetable garden. My father always was a poor huntsman. At first, we grated our corn until my father hollowed out a log and we ground it, as in a mortar. We had no cooking-stove, of course, and baked our bread in the only skillet we possessed. The ripe corn was boiled until it was soft, then grated and baked. The nearest mill was thirty miles off.

As I have already said, the country was very thinly settled. Our three neighbors, Burnett, Dougherty, and Sutherland, lived in a radius of seven miles. San Felipe was twenty-eight miles off, and there were about two houses on the road thither. In consequence, there was no market for anything you could raise, except for cigars and tobacco, which my father was the first in Texas to put on the market. He sold them in San Felipe to a Frenchman, D'Orvanne,[52][53] who had a store there, but this was several years afterwards.

We raised barely what we needed, and we kept it. Around San Felipe certainly it was different, and there were some beautiful farms in the vicinity.

Before the war, there was a school in Washington, taught by a Miss Trest, where the Daughertys sent their daughter, boarding her in the city. Of course, we did not patronize it.

We lived in our doorless and windowless six-cornered pavilion about three years.

---

52  [This man's full name was Alexander Bourgeois D'Orvanne. He afterwards played a prominent part in the founding of the German colonies of New Braunfels and Fredericksburg in 1843-46 by the *Mainzer Adelsverein*. See *Entwicklungsgeschichte der Deutschen Kolonie Friedrichsburg* by Robert Penniger, Fredericksburg, Texas, 1896. Mrs. Rosa Kleberg tells me that her party was very hospitably entertained by him when they were on their way from Harrisburg to their farm at Cat Spring in 1835. He had a fine general mercantile business. He impressed her as a very estimable gentleman. — R. K., Jr.]

53  In his novel, Deutsche Suchen den Garten der Welt - Der Schicksal deutscher Auswanderer in Texas vor 100 Jahren, EPubli 2017 (ISBN: 978-3745082579), the author, Fritz Scheffel puts Alexander Bourgeois D'Orvanne in a much less favorable light. (Ed.)

Life of German Pioneers in Early Texas.                                    185

When the war broke out, my father at first intended quietly to remain at his home. But the Mexicans had induced the Kickapoo Indians to revolt, and he was warned by Captains Lester, York, and Pettus against the savages. We then set out with the intention of crossing the Sabine and seeking safety in the States. When we arrived at the Brazos, we found so many people assembled at the ferry that it would have been three days before the one small ferry-boat could have carried us over the stream. The roads were almost impassable. So my father pitched his camp in the middle of the Brazos bottom near Brenham. Here we remained until after the Battle of San Jacinto.

Thirteen men with their families, mostly Münsterländers and Oldenburgers from Cummins Creek, were in our party. They were Amsler, Weppler, Captain Vrek, Bartels, Damke, Wolters, Piefer, Boehmen, Schneider, Kleekemp, Kasper, Heimann, Gründer, and Witte.

Some of the Germans fared ill on account of their tardy flight. Mrs. Goegens and her children were captured by the Indians and taken to the border of Texas, where American traders ransomed the lady, but had not sufficient money to purchase the children. These remained with the Indians. The Mexicans captured Stoehlke and intended to hang him. Upon his using the name of Jesus Christ, they released him. Kaspar Simon was also made a prisoner, but released upon exhibiting his ignorance of the whereabouts of the Texan army.

After the war, times were hard. However, my father had buried a good many things and had in this way succeeded in keeping them from the Mexicans He had placed two posts a considerable distance apart, and had buried his treasures just midway between them. The posts had both been pulled out and holes dug near them, but our things had not been found. Our house and garden had been left unharmed, though those of our neighbors had been destroyed. The explanation of this is probably to be found in the fact that the Münsterländers, who were

Catholics, had brought all their holy relics to our place and had set up several crosses in our garden.

Just as we had returned from the "runaway scrape," and had scarcely unhitched our horses, Vrels came running up and told us that a party of Mexicans had taken his horse. Ellison, York, and John Pettus, who had just returned from the army, galloped after the robbers, and, after York had killed one of them, recovered the horse.

We had plenty of corn and bacon. My brother and John Pettus brought back a few of our cattle from Gonzales. Before the war, there had been very little trouble; but afterwards, there was a good deal of fighting in our neighborhood, especially about election time. A short time afterwards, my father began keeping a boardinghouse and had a large building constructed for that purpose. He tore down the six-cornered pavilion, over the protest of my mother, who wanted to keep it as a sort of memento of former days. Many German immigrants accordingly came to our house. Nearly all managed very badly at first, using all their money before they had learned to accommodate themselves to their new surroundings.

Industry was founded about this time and named by Benninghoffer after a lively dispute. My father was justice of the peace for quite a time, and later was engaged in general merchandising.

I remember very well the coming of the German colonists who founded New Braunfels and Fredericksburg. My brother Fritz accompanied Solms[54] in the capacity of interpreter and guide. The prince had a considerable retinue of horsemen, dressed mostly like himself, after the fashion of German officers. Among the company were an architect, a cook, and a professional hunter (jaeger). Whenever they came to a good piece of road, the prince would, say, "Now let us gallop," and then the whole party would charge down the prairie. The hunter was com-

---

54  Prince Carl of Solms-Braunfels, Commissioner General of the *Adelsverein*. (Ed.)

manded to kill a deer, but did not succeed, and my brother rode out and killed one, causing much pleasure to the prince.

While on the same journey, the party stopped at a farmer's, who brought out watermelons and told them to help themselves. My brother cut a watermelon in two, took a piece, and went out into the yard to eat, whereupon one of the officers rebuked him severely, asking him how he could dare to eat when His Highness had not yet tasted.

When the prince was endeavoring to establish the Karlshafen (Indianola), and he and his party were making soundings, the boat grounded. The prince was in great distress and insisted that the only thing to do was to wait for the tide. My brother then took off his clothes, got out, and pushed the boat off the sandbank.

I also remember that the prince's cook came to my mother for information in regard to Texas dishes.

I lived in Industry until I married Louis von Roeder. Nearly all my time was spent in attending to our household, and I had little opportunity for traveling about. I was not in San Felipe after the war.

[This narrative has been prepared for publication in *The Quarterly* by Rudolph Kleberg, Jr. See *Quarterly* for April, 1898, p. 297[55], and for October, 1898, p. 170[56]. — Editor Quarterly.]

---

55  Kleberg, Rudolf, Jr. *Some of my Early Experiences in Texas I – Rosa Kleberg*, Southwestern Historical Quarterly Online Vol. 001, Issue 4, p. 297. 1898. Accessed Sepember 1. 2017.
56  Kleberg, Rudolf, Jr. *Some of my Early Experiences in Texas II – Rosa Kleberg*, Southwestern Historical Quarterly Online Vol 002, Issue 2, p. 170. 1898. https://texashistory.unt.edu/ark:/67531/metapth101011/m1/174/. Accessed Sepember 1. 2017.

# Robert Justus Kleberg, Yorktown.

Robert Justus Kleberg (christened Johnun Christian Justus Robert Kleberg), was born on the 10th day of September, A. D. 1803, in Herstelle, Westphalia, in the former Kingdom of Prussia. His parents were Lucas Kleberg, a prominent and successful merchant, and Veronica Kleberg (nee Meier) a lady of fine culture, sweet temper and good sense. They moved from Herstelle to Beverungen in Westphalia, where they were quite prosperous for a time. Besides Robert they had the following children: Ernest, Louis, Joseph and Banise. For a number of years Robert's parents, living in affluent circumstances, were permitted to give their children good educational advantages, but unhappily misfortune and death deprived the children at an early age of kind parental protection, and the subject of this sketch was thrown upon his own resources, which consisted chiefly of a healthy mind and body, a strong will and unsullied name. At an early age he entered the Gymnasium of Holzminden, where after a five years' course in the classics he completed his studies with high honors. Choosing the law as his profession he now entered the University of Goettingen, and in two years and a half received his diploma as *doctor juris*. Soon after he was appointed as one of the justices of the assizes of Nirhiem, where he remained one year, after which he was promoted to various judicial positions, in which he prepared himself for the practice of his profession, and In which he served with credit and distinction.

In 1834 when he was about ready to enter upon a distinguished judicial career, he concluded to emigrate to the United States. His reason for this sudden and important change in his life can best be found in his own language, which is taken from a memorandum of his own writing:--

"I wished to live under a Republican form of government, with unbounded personal, religious and political liberty, free from the petty tyrannies, the many disadvantages and evils of old countries. Prussia, my former home, smarted at the time under a military despotism. I was (and have ever remained) an enthusiastic lover of republican institutions, and I expected to find in Texas, above all other countries, the blessed land of my most fervent hopes."

Texas was yet partially unexplored, but the reports that reached the old country were of the most extravagant and romantic nature, and were well calculated to enthuse the impulsive and courageous spirit of the young referendary. The ardor of his desires to emigrate was heightened by a letter written by a Mr. Ernst, a German from the Duchy of Oldenburg, who had emigrated to Texas a few years previous, and who at that time resided in what is now known as Industry, Austin County, Texas. This letter recited the advantages of Texas in the most glowing colors, comparing its climate to the sunny skies of Italy; it lauded the fertility of the soil and spoke of the perennial flora of the prairies of Texas, etc. About this time, September the 4th, 1834, the subject of this sketch married Miss Rosalia von Roeder, daughter of Lieut. Ludwig Anton Siegmund von Roeder, the head of an old family of nobility who, too, were anxious for the same reasons to emigrate to Texas. The party had first contemplated to emigrate to one of the Western States of the United States, but it was now determined to go to Texas. Again, the memorandum above referred to runs as follows:—

"We changed our first intention to go to one of the Western States, and chose Texas for our future home. As soon as this was determined upon we sent some of our party, to wit, three brothers of my wife, unmarried, Louis, Albrecht and Joachim, and their sister Valesca, and a servant by the name of Pollhart, ahead of us to Texas for the purpose of selecting a point where we could all meet and commence operations. They were well provided with money, clothing, a light wagon and harness, tools, and generally everything necessary to commence a settlement. They aimed to go to Mr. Ernst, the writer of the letter which induced us to go to Texas. Six months after our party had left the old country, and shortly after we had received the news of their safe arrival, we followed on the last day of September, A. D. 1834, in the ship 'Congress,' Capt. J. Adams."

The party consisted of Robert Kleberg and wife, Lieut. L. A. S. v. Roeder and wife, his daughters, Louise and Caroline, his sons, Rudolph, Otto and William v. Roeder, Louis Kleberg, Mrs. Otto v. Roeder, nee Pauline von Donop and Miss Antoinette von Donop (afterwards wife of Rudolph von Roeder). The other passengers were nearly all Germans from Oldenburg, and one of them was the brother-in-law of Mr. Ernst. They were all bound for the same point in Texas, and after a voyage of sixty days landed in New Orleans.

The narrative of said memorandum here proceeds: —

"Here we heard very bad accounts about Texas, and we were advised not to go to Texas, which it was said was infested with robbers, murderers and wild Indians. But we were determined to risk it, and could not disappoint our friends who had preceded us. As soon, therefore, as we succeeded in chartering the schooner 'Sabin,' about two weeks after we landed in New Orleans, we sailed for Brazoria, Texas. After a voyage of eight days we wrecked off of Galveston Island, December 22d, 1834. The 'Sabin' was an American craft of about 150 tons. The captain and crew left the island, I think, in the steamer, 'Ocean.' The wreck was sold in Brazoria at public auction and bought by a gentleman who had come in the 'Ocean,' for thirty-odd dollars. Perhaps she was not regularly employed in the trade between New Orleans and Texas, and was only put in order to get her wrecked in order to get the amount for which she was insured. This was the opinion of the passengers at the time. It is impossible for me to name with certainty the exact point of the island at which we stranded, but I think it was not far from the center of the island, about ten miles above the present site of the city; it was on the beach side. The island was a perfect wilderness and inhabited only by deer, wolves and rattlesnakes. All the passengers were safely brought to shore, and were provided with provisions, partly from those on board ship and partly by the game on the island. Most of the men were delighted with the climate on the island, and the sport they enjoyed by hunting or fishing. A committee of five was appointed to ascertain whether we were on an island or on main land. After an investigation of two days the committee reported that we were on an island. The passengers then went regularly into camp, saving all the goods and provisions from the wrecked vessel, which was only about fifty yards from shore. From the sails, masts and beams they constructed a large tent, with separate compartments for women and children. Thus the passengers were temporarily protected against the inclemency of the weather. Two or three days after our vessel had sunk the steamer 'Ocean' hove in sight and, observing our signal of distress, anchored opposite our camp and sent a boat ashore with an officer to find out the situation. The captain would not take all the passengers, but consented to take a few, charging them a doubloon each. I, with Rudolph v. Roeder, took passage on the steamer, which was bound for Brazoria. I went as agent of the remaining passengers to charter a boat to take them and their plunder to the main land. Finding no boat at Brazoria, or Bell's Landing, the only Texas ports at that time, I proceeded on foot to San Felipe, where I was told I would find a small steamer, the 'Cuyuga,' Capt. W. Harris. I found the steamer, but did not succeed in chartering her, the price asked ($1,000) being too high.

"In San Felipe I heard for the first time of the whereabouts of my relatives, who had preceded us. Here I also formed the acquaintance of Col. Frank Johnson and Capt. Mosely Baker, under whose command I afterwards participated in the battle of San Jacinto. These gentlemen informed me that two of my friends, Louis and Albert von Roeder, had located about fourteen miles from San Felipe on a league and labor of land, but that Joachim and Valesca von Roeder had died. We found them in a miserable hut and in a pitiful condition. They were emaciated by disease and want, and without money. Tears of joy streamed from their eyes when they beheld us. After a few days rest I continued my errand to charter a boat. I had a letter of introduction to Stephen F. Austin and Sam Williams from a merchant in New Orleans to whom our ship had been consigned, which I presented to Mr. Austin's private secretary, Mr. Austin and Mr. Williams being absent. From him I received a letter of introduction to Mr. Scott, the father-in-law of Mr. Williams. From Mr. Scott I finally succeeded in chartering a small vessel for $100.00 for three trips, and immediately returned to Galveston, landing on the bay side opposite the camp four weeks after I had left it. I found the passengers of the old 'Sabin' in good health and spirits. They had spent their time in hunting and fishing. Those who could not shoot were employed to drive the deer to the hunters. There were deer by the thousands. I left the next day with the first cargo of passengers, including my wife, her parents and Caroline von Roeder. After a stormy trip we arrived on the evening of the same day at Mr. Scott's place, where we were hospitably treated. The next day we reached Harrisburg, where I succeeded in renting a comfortable house, intending to remain there until all the passengers had arrived from the island. The last passengers did not arrive until the winter of 1835, though had I hired another small sloop from Capt. Smith in Velasco, which also made three trips. The winter of 1835 was unusually severe."

This, it seems, ended the eventful and lengthy voyage from the old country to Texas, of which only the main incidents are given, to show the difficulties and many privations to which Texas emigrants in those early days were subjected.

Robert Kleberg, by reason of his superior education, was the only one among those early German colonists who could make himself understood to the few American pioneers who inhabited the interior, and acted as spokesman for the rest. Indian tribes, both savage and civil, swarmed through the country, and it was necessary for the colonists to explore and settle the country in communities for self-defense. This condition of things is apparent from the narrative, which relates:—

"To the place which had been settled upon by Louis and Albrecht v. Roeder we now repaired, leaving the ladies and children in Harrisburg, under the protection of one of the gentlemen. We had formed a partnership with the view of assisting each other to cultivate farms and build houses for each head of a family in our party, and we were to work in good earnest to break up land and fence it, and to build houses, as it was our intention to move the balance of our party from Harrisburg to our new settlement as soon as we could erect houses, but not being accustomed to manual labor, we proceeded very slowly. There was an Indian tribe, the Kikapoos, encamped on our land about a mile from our camp, who furnished us with game of all kinds, which the country afforded in abundance. The squaws were very useful to us, as they would hunt and bring in camp our oxen and horses when they strayed off. We rewarded them with ammunition and trinkets, which we had brought with us for that purpose.

"We had supplied ourselves with everything necessary to commence a settlement in a new country. We had wagons, farming implements, all sorts of tools, household and kitchen furniture, and clothing which we had brought with us from Germany. Early in September, 1835, we had finished building two log houses, one of them had even a floor and ceiling, as we had sawed by hand the planks from post-oak trees. We had also inclosed and planted a field of ten acres in corn and cotton, and we now moved the members of our party who had remained at Harrisburg to our settlement, with our wagons and teams. Such of our goods, for which we had no room, or no immediate use, we left at the house which we had rented at Harrisburg. Among the objects we left was a fine piano, belonging to my wife, many valuable oil paintings and engravings, music books, etc., all of which fell a prey to the flames which consumed Harrisburg during the war, which followed in the following spring."

Many were the privations and severe the task which these early settlers had already undergone in permanently settling in the adopted country, but their trials had only begun; the furies of war threatened to devastate the settlements of the colonies, and Santa Anna was marching his minions into Texas to destroy the constitutional liberty of her people, and Texas patriots, though few in number, bore up her flag to rescue it from thralldom. Among them we find Robert Kleberg and his brother-in-law and compatriots. Albert and Louis von Roeder had participated in the sanguinary storming of San Antonio and returned to their settlement near San Felipe, when in the spring of 1836 occurred the massacre of Goliad and the fall of the Alamo. Texas independence bad been proclaimed, Santa Anna was preparing his march of conquest to the Sabine, when the young Republic, under her noble leader, Sam Houston, was making her last patriotic appeal to her bravest sons, in whose hearts were now gathered all the hopes of Texas. It was at this juncture that at a family meeting of the Roeders and Klebergs, presided over by Ex-Lieut. Von Roeder, that these distressed colonists held a counsel of war to decide whether to fight for Texas independence, or cross her borders into the older States to seek shelter under the protecting aegis of the American eagle. The meeting was held under the sturdy oaks that stood on the newly acquired possessions. It was a supreme moment in the lives of those who participated. In the language of the historian: "The flight of the wise and worthy men of the country from danger, tended to frighten the old, young and helpless, furnished excuses to the timid, and sanctioned the course of the cowardly. The general dismay following the adjournment of the convention, induced many brave men impelled irresistibly by natural impulses to go to their abandoned fugitive wives and children, to tender them protection." This little band, like their compatriots, found themselves in the midst of a terrible panic and they were now called upon to decide between love of country and love of self and it may well be presumed that the debates in this little convention were of a stormy nature. The subject of our sketch, though bound by the strongest ties of love to an affectionate young wife and her infant child, was the champion of Texas liberty, and it was due to the eloquent and impassioned appeals of himself and the venerable presiding officer that it was decided that the party would remain, and share the fate of the heroic few who had rallied under San Houston to fight for the independence of Texas against Mexican despotism. As Albrecht v. Roeder and Louis v. Roeder had just returned battle-worn from the bloody fields of San Antonio de Bexar, they and others, except L. v. Roeder, were detailed under the aged Ex-Lieut. Roeder to remain with the fugitive families while Robert Kleberg, Louis v. Roeder and Otto v. Roeder were chosen to bear the brunt of battle. Now a parting, possibly for life, from all that was dear on earth and a voluntary march in the ranks of Capt. Mosley Baker's Company was the next act in the drama of our warrior's life and, while the curtain fell on the pathetic scene, a brave young wife mounted a Texas pony with her tender babe to go with the rest of the Texas families to perhaps across the borders of Texas, driving before them the cattle and horses of the colonists. The acts and deeds of Robert Kleberg from this time to the disbanding of the Texas army of patriots are a part and parcel of the history of Texas. Endowed with a spirit of patriotism which bordered on the sublime, possessed of a healthy and robust physical constitution, a cultured, polished, cool and discriminating mind, he despised fear and was anxious to engage in the sanguinary and decisive struggle for freedom which culminated so gloriously for Texas and civilization on the historic field of San Jacinto. After this memorable battle, in which he and Louis v. Roeder participated to the glory of themselves and their posterity, he was with Gen. Rusk and the Texas van guard following the vanquished armies of Santa Anna to the Mexican border and, returning by Goliad, assisted in the sad obsequies of the remains of Fannin and his brave men. In the meantime his family had moved back to Galveston Island, and we will again draw from the memorandum for the better appreciation and understanding of the conditions of the country that prevailed at this time: "It had been the intention of our party who went to Galveston Island in the absence of those who were in the army, to abandon the settlement commenced on the Brazos and settle on the island on the two leagues which were chosen there. This move had been undertaken in my absence, partly from fear or danger from hostile Indians, also a want of provisions, and partly with an idea to permanently settle on the island. For that purpose the party had built a boat of about forty tons in order to move our cattle and horses and other property from the mainland. They were ignorant of the laws of Mexico, which reserved the islands for the government." To show the state of civilization on Galveston Island at that time, in the summer of 1836, the judge relates the following incident which occurred while he was in the army: 'One night during a time when all were enwrapt in sound slumber, they were suddenly aroused by the frantic cries of one of the ladies of the party, Mrs. L. Kleberg; she was so frightened that she could not speak, but only screamed, pointing her finger to a huge, dark object close to the head of the pallet upon which lay my wife and Mrs. Otto v. Roeder and their babes. To their great astonishment they discovered it to be an immense alligator, his jaws wide open, making for the children to devour them. Mr. v. Roeder, Sr., and Mr. Chas. Mason, who had hastened to the spot, dispatched the monster with fire and sword.'"

The narrative, speaking of their residence on the island after Mr. Kleberg returned from the war, proceeds: "We remained about three months on the island after building our house. Most of us were sick, especially the women and children — long exposure, bad food and water were the probable causes. Not long after we moved into the house, Mrs. Pauline Roeder, wife of Otto v. Roeder, died there. We buried her under the 'Three Lone Trees.' We were all down with chills and fever. Four Mexican prisoners waited on us. Their principal occupation was to gather oysters, pack wood from the beach of the gulf, make fires, wash dishes and clothing, and pack the deer which Mr. v. Roeder and myself killed, which, together with the fish and oysters, was our chief means of subsistence. We had neither bread nor coffee, nor sugar, and the water, of course, was brackish. Finally under these distressing circumstances we became despondent and disheartened ; so, late in October, 1836, we again boarded our boat, taking along every thing we had with us, including our Mexican prisoners, who acted as oarsmen, and once more made for the main land, landing at a place called Liverpool, a small village at the head of Chocolate bayou. The house on Galveston Island was abandoned, there being no one to whom we could sell; there were no other families at that time residing on the island. Only Morgan's Fort was situated near the east end of Galveston Island. There were about 400 Mexican prisoners held there. Capt. Turner, Col. Morgan, and Judge Chas. Mason were there, but no families that I recollect."

The colonists, including the subject of this sketch, again located where they had made the first settlement, at a point known as Cat Spring, now in Austin County. This was in the month of November, 1836. Here Judge Kleberg and his family resided until the fall of 1847, when they removed to DeWitt County. At Cat Spring were born the following of his children: Clara Siegesmunde, November 28, 1835; Johanna Caroline, November 29, 1838; Caroline Louise, January 15, 1840, and Otto Joseph, October 27, 1841; Rudolph, June 26, 1847. In DeWitt County, Marcellus Eugene, February 7, 1849; Robt. Justus, December 5, 1853, and Louise Rosalie, September 2, 1855.

While living in Austin County, Judge Kleberg did much to develop the new country, which was then but sparsely settled, and was still inhabited by Indians. He frequently spoke of one occurrence during his residence at Cat Spring, where a numerous tribe of Comanches passed by his house to the city of Houston to interview the President of the Republic of Texas on the question of making peace. He speaks of the appearance of these savages upon their return from Houston as most ludicrous. Many of them had adorned themselves with stove pipe hats, red ribbons and all kinds of fancy dress articles, all of which was in strange contrast with their usual wearing apparel. They stopped at the Judge's house on their way from Houston, and requested his wife to mend their flag, which she readily consented to do. Being well acquainted with the prominent citizens such as Sam Houston, Burnet, J. S. Hill, J. P. Borden, Judge Waller, and many other distinguished citizens of that day, Mr. Kleberg's services in the War for Independence and his ability were soon recognized by the young Republic and as early as 1837 he was appointed by President Sam Houston as Associate Commissioner of the Board of Land Commissioners. In 1838, he was appointed President of said commissioners by J. P. Borden, Commissioner of the General Land Office. In 1841, he was commissioned by Mirabeau B. Lamar, President of the Republic, Justice of the Peace, which was then an important office as there were few lawyers, and few law books, and important and perplexing suits to be decided in these courts. In 1846 he was elected Chief Justice in Austin County, and commissioned by Sam Houston, Governor. In 1848 he was elected County Commissioner of De Witt County, and commissioned by Governor G. S. Wood.

In 1853 he was elected Chief Justice of De Witt County, and commissioned by Governor Bell. He was re-elected as Chief Justice of De Witt County in 1854. When the war broke out he became a strong Confederate and raised a company of militia, but was on account of his advanced age not received in active service, but finally commissioned as collector of war taxes, which position he occupied during the entire period of the war, and administered with skill and fidelity. After the war he accepted the situation and filled several positions of trust and honor, such as member of the county school board, etc. Upon his arrival in De Witt he found but few settlers, among them the following prominent citizens: John Pettus, the Yorks and Bells, Judges Wofford and Baker, Dr. Robert Peobles, Capt. Dick

Chrisholm, Judge Young and others. At that time there were hardly any schools and churches in De Witt County and Judge Kleberg, together with Messrs. Albrecht v. Roeder, John Pettus, the Bells, and Yorks, erected with their own hands a log cabin on the Colita creek, near the old York and Bell farm, which was probably the first school-house in the county.

Hostile Indians still made their accustomed raids on the settlements and as late as October, 1848, the pioneers of De Witt County had a fight with the savages, in which Judge Kleberg participated, and of which he gives the following account:—

"One October morning Capt. York and Mr. Albrecht v. Roeder and my brother, Ernst Kleberg, summoned me to go with a party of volunteers to fight a tribe of hostile Indians, who were depredating in the neighborhood of Yorktown. We were soon mounted and equipped and off for the place of rendezvous. We reached the Cabesa that same night, where our troops, consisting of some thirty men, camped and elected Capt. York as commander, and Messrs. William Taylor, Jno. Thomlinson and Rufus Taylor were detailed as spies and skirmishers. Next morning the company, as organized, started to meet the foe, whom we encountered about three o'clock p.m. on the Escondido east of the San Antonio river, about fifteen miles west of the present town of Yorktown, just as our company filed around a point of timber. The Indians, about sixty to seventy strong, lay in ambush. Our company was not marching in rank and file, but in an irregular way, not expecting to meet the enemy so soon. Capt. York and Mr. Bell were in front, followed immediately by John Pettus and myself. The Indians raised the well-known and hideous war-whoop and immediately opened on us with a terrible fire of musketry. The majority of our men took to flight and left not more than ten or twelve of us, who made a stand, taking advantage of a little grove near by, where the Texians returned a sharp fire upon the Indians, who still remained in ambush, only exposing their heads now and then as they fired, thus having a decided advantage over the men who were only protected by a few thin trees. It was here that Mr. Bell and Capt. York were killed. The former, a son-in-law of Capt. York, was shot at the first fire and mortally wounded, but he was carried along to the little mott, where Capt. York and myself bent over him to dress his wounds, but he died in our hands. At this juncture Mr. Jim York, son of Capt. York, was shot in the head. Capt. York called me to assist him in dressing his son's wounds. I tore off a piece of his shirt and bandaged his wounds as well as possible. Capt. York, overcome by grief, ran continually from his son to his son-in-law, and thus exposed himself to the fire of the enemy, notwithstanding I kept warning him, and was soon struck by the fatal ball which instantly killed him. A counsel of war was now held by the remaining troops, consisting of eight or nine men all told, and we decided to proceed to a little mound or elevation near by, where we might flank the Indians in their ambush. In attempting to gain this point the Indians kept up a continuous fusillade, which we returned, and by the time we reached the elevation and directed our fire from behind a cluster of large live oaks on the exposed flank of the savages, they soon retired from their position and disappeared from the field. Thus ended probably the last Indian fight in Southwest Texas, and such were the stirring scenes of that time."

Mr. Kleberg had the good fortune to outlive this period of romance and adventure, and to see his adopted State and country developed to grand proportions in population and wealth under the magic wand of civilization.

In politics Judge Kleberg was always a consistent and intelligent Democrat; a strong believer in State rights and local self-government, and an ardent admirer of the American system of government, and in his severest trials as an early settler, and in the gloomiest hour of the Republic and State of his adoption he never faltered in his faith in the free institutions of this country, and spurned the idea of returning to a monarchical form of government. In religion he was free of all orthodoxy and most tolerant to all denominations; candid and firm in his individual convictions, yet respectful and considerate of the opinions of others. Pure and lofty in sentiment, simple and frugal in habit, honest in motive, and positive and decided in word and deed, his character was without reproach, and indeed a model among his fellow-men.

Mr. Kleberg was a man of deep and most varied learning. Besides a knowledge of Greek and Latin he controlled three modern languages and read their literatures in the originals. Reading and study were a part of his daily life, and he enjoyed a critical and discriminating knowledge of ancient and modern literature. In field and camp and the solitudes of frontier life his well-trained mind ever found delight and repose in the contemplation of its ample stores of knowledge and the graces of a refined civilization under which it was developed were never effaced, or even blurred by the roughness or crudities of border life. A man of urbane manners and courtly address, his intercourse with men, whether high or low, educated or ignorant, was ever characterized by a plain and noble dignity, free of assumption or vanity.

The principles which found expression and exemplification in his long and eventful life rested upon a broad and comprehensive philosophy of which absolute honesty of mind was a controlling element, and when the shadows of death gathered around him he met the supreme moment with a mind serene and in peaceful composure. He died at Yorktown, De Witt County, October 23, 1888, in his eighty-sixth year, surrounded by his family, and was buried with Masonic honors. His wife, Mrs. Rosa Kleberg, and the following children survive him: Mrs. Clara Hillebrand, Mrs. Caroline Eckhardt, Miss Lulu Kleberg, Hon. Rudolph Kleberg, Marcellus E. Kleberg, and Robert J. Kleberg.

His eldest son, Otto Kleberg, who served with distinction in the Confederate army, preceded him in death in 1880.

Article taken from *Indian Wars and Pioneers of Texas by John Henry Brown, 1820-1895*. Austin: L.E. Daniel 1890.

# The First German Woman in Texas

## Louise Ernst Stoehr[57]

These are the memoirs of Louise Ernst Stoehr[58], wife of Friedrich Ernst, founder of the first German settlement in Texas. They were first published as "Die Erst Deutsch Frau in Texas" in 1884 in Deutsch Pioneer. She was in her mid 80's when she wrote this article, a half-century after the events she recounted; some of her statements contain known errors and exaggerations. Fortunately her daughter Caroline Ernst von Roeder Hinueber wrote her own memoirs about the same time, covering much of the same account as her mother gave, although more extensively and more accurately. Together the two present a fascinating story of a truly pioneer family experience. Crystal Rasgdale, in The Golden Free Land, has added notes to this account, editing and providing more detail.

"I was born on July 30, 1800, in the town of Oldenburg, Germany, and was married at the age of about twenty years to Mr. Fritz Ernst[59] from Barel, Grostherzogthum, Oldenburg. In the fall of 1827[60] my husband made the decision to emigrate to America, a decision that he immediately carried out. After a

---

57 Stoehr, Louise Ernst, *Die Erste Deutsch Frau in Texas*, Deutsch Pioneer 16 (1884): 372 - 375.
58 She was born as Luise Weber (*Das Silbernen Buch der Familie Sack* – Sack'sche Familienstiftung, 2010)
59 Friedrich Ernst was born in 1796. Ibid.
60 According to the records held by the Sack Family, they actually emigrated from Le Havre in France in 1829.

stormy passage we landed in New York in the winter of the same year, where we immediately established a hotel, a business that proved to be prosperous. My husband was acquainted with the rich old Astor, a honest German man, who suggested to my husband to start a modern dairy farm; he would sell him a ten acre tract for a few thousand dollars along the East River, where even now Wall Street lies and would give him time to repay it in increments. Through this Ernst would have become a multimillionaire, since the stock exchange is on this street today and land can hardly be bought with money. Although I advised my husband to take this offer, he did not accept my advice; instead, he decided to go to Mexico in February, 1831, in particular to the province of Texas.

"Thus we sailed with the Mexican schooner Saltillo and arrived on April 21, 1831, in Harrisburg, Texas. This spot consisted at that time of about twenty houses or, better, huts: the present state capital of Houston did not even exist by name, and then in the main seaport of Galveston one didn't dare to land because of fear of the Karankawa Indians, who at that time inhabited the island.

"From Harrisburg we continued by ox-cart to the town of San Felipe de Austin, located fifty miles to the west. The latter had 300-400 inhabitants, among whom we found a German by the name of Wertzner, who engaged in the noble tailoring business. Wertzner is thus the first German man who set foot on Texas soil. He died in the fortieth year in Biegel's Settlement. Here we now sat on the edge of all civilization, because just westerly the Indians lived, and no white man had ever before crossed Mill Creek. My husband undertook from here inspection tours in order to select some land, and thus he also came to the forks of the creek, where now Industry is located, and since the location because of its romantic, its beautiful waters and the woods pleased my husband, he had one league of land surveyed by the Mexican land commissioner, who had his chancellory in San Felipe. We built a log house about two hundred feet below here, where I still live today, and furnished it in the best possible way. Some months later we sold one quarter of our land for ten or twelve milk cows. At least now we had milk and butter. Meat was available through the abundant wild life, and some bushels of 'Welsh' grain which we had brought from San Felipe, which gave us bread until we had our first harvest.

"Now, Mr. Charles Fordtran lived a mile west of us; this gentleman came here with us. To the north we had no neighbors up to the White River in the Union State Arkansas, to the east to the Saline river, and to the south none up to San Felipe. The entire surroundings which lie before you now covered with fam settlements and towns were then a waving prairie on which thousands of buffalo and other wildlife roamed. Like this we lived all alone in the wilderness; it seemed to be lonesome even for the Indians, in the years 1831 and 1832. They visited us a few times, and particularly as soon as they found out that we were Germans, they approached us in a friendly manner, and often times brought back our runaway horses and cows in return for a little milk and butter. There existed no form of money then, and there was only trade. Through the efforts of Mr. Fordtran German immigrants were brought here in the fall of 1833. Among these were the families Bartels, Zimmerscheit and Jurgens. In the next year the following families arrived here. Karl Amsler, Wolters, Kleberg, Frels, von Roeder, Siebel, Grassmetyer, and others whose names escape me. In the same year also the first troop of Anglo-Americans came to this area and settled about thirty miles to the north at the New Years Creek.

"Up until the fall of 1834 only four American families had settled down in our immediate neighborhood, namely Joe Robison, eight miles from here at the Buffalo Creek; Sutherland; Captain Jack; and Burnett. This strong surge of whites roused the Indians and now they didn't come anymore as before in a friendly manner, rather, they began to bother us with the driving off of our horses and cattle; because of this often-times bloody encounters occurred.

"The first white to be killed by Indians was Mr. Joe Robison, father of Colonel Joel Robison, who still lives today near Warrenton. In the fall of the same year the redskins stole the wife and two children of Mr. Jurgens, who had settled down four miles from here at Post Oak Point. The Catholic missionaries, however, were able to free Mrs. Jurgens from the hands of the Indians, but of the children nothing was heard ever again.

"The year 1835 brought us the Texas liberation war with Mexico, and since we didn't feel safe here any longer, we moved to the denser populated settlement at New Years Creek. We stayed there until after the decisive San Jacinto battle. We returned to our homestead to find nothing remaining of our property but rubble and ashes. The State of Texas has, however, done nothing up to date to compensate us in the least way for our loss, even though my husband in the matter of Texas emancipation served in the ranks of the Texan army, and I myself gave everything. "The land settlement gained momentum now and brought several hundred Germans here between the years of 1838 and 1842. In 1842 we had the honor to be visited by the pioneers of the German Emigration Association: Prince Solms-Braunfels, Count Boos von Waldeck, and Prince von Leiningen. The gentleman had an idea to convert Texas into a German colony and to organize a monarchy here.

"My husband assured them that this would prove to be a difficult task, since there was too much republican feeling in the air here, and that such an attempt would never be accepted by the neighboring American republic. From here they continued on to see Mr. Fordtran and bought, if I am not mistaken, through his mediation, a stretch of land which they later christened 'Farm Nassau', from which colony New Braunfels was supplied with provisions.[61]

"The first years of our settling have rooted themselves so deeply in my mind that I shall never be able to forget them. I can still

---

61  See Nassau Plantation: *The Evolution of a Texas German Slave Plantation* by James C. Kearney, (Denton, University of North Texas Press, 2010).

see the Indians clearly in front of me as they once leisurely killed and ate in front of our eyes our only oxen, and also, shall I never forget as the Mexicans, fleeing from the battlefield of San Jacinto, butchered our best milk cow. "The name of my eldest son is Herman Ernst, and he lives about a mile from here; he is sixty-three years old. The other sons died after their father, who died in 1858. My two daughters are still living, and you are seeing one in front of you. She is the widowed Wilhelmine Schroeder, and she has eight children and more than thirty grandchildren. She is sixty-one years old. I am living with her since the time my second husband, Mr. Stohr, died. My second daughter's name is Caroline Hinueber, widowed von Roeder[62], and she lives near Meyersville in De Witt district."

---

62 She actually married Carl Ludwig "Louis" Socrates von Roeder on 21 May 1837 and he died in 1840. In this short marriage, she managed to bear three children, Louis, Maria and Ernst von Roeder. She then married his younger brother Franz Ferdinand Albrecht Albert Ludwig von Roeder in 1841 by whom she had eight children. He died in 1857. (Records of the Sack Family). In 1861 she married Werner von Hinueber with who she had twins. (TSHA).

# Excerpts from *Experiences and Observations*

The following are selections from William Trenckmann's series of supplements to his newspaper Das Wochenblat, between 1931 and 1893, that describe his life as the son of a German immigrant to Texas, his career as an educator and a German newspaperman. Trenckmann's work has been republished on amazon.com in 2015 by James Woodrick.

## MILLHEIM AND ITS SCHOOL

For long years the conviction has been growing in me that the region in which a person grows up influences him both physically and mentally. I have had this conviction confirmed in my present surroundings as well as in the past when I compared the "Sandhasen" (sand hares) of the Bernard Prairie with their kinsmen who grew up on the black hilly land around Shelby or between Mill Creek and the Brazos. I noted differences between those who grew up on the "Hog Wallow Prairie" and those of the Brazos Bottom. That difference did not consist only in the fact that the inhabitants of the sandy prairie averaged a few inches taller in height than the others. Later in Travis County I found similar differences between the hill folks from our cedar brakes and the folks from Pflugerville, Dessau and Richland. Therefore I believe that I should tell something about Millheim, where my cradle stood, if I ever had a cradle. If I had one, it was soon given away because I was the youngest in my family. Cradles were in great demand in Old Millheim, where a dozen children per family were no rare exception.

Millheim was the third oldest of the solid German settlements in Austin County. Even before the first German settler, Louis Kleberg, settled there at the beginning of the 1840's, Anglo-American squatters, who came there because things were getting too crowded for them on the other side of the Mississippi, had settled north of Millheim in the extensive forest on the southwest side of Mill Creek. They had built log cabins in a clearing, had probably planted a small patch of corn for bread, and had lived chiefly in a great abundance of game. One of them, more industrious than the rest, is even said to have planted fruit trees. When the Germans arrived, these squatters had already moved on. San Felipe, which was to become the capital of Austin's Colony, was too near to suit them. A few years before Kleberg, two Anglo-American farmers - Swearingen and Clark - who really liked hunting better than farming, had settled near the edge of the flat prairie. They soon became good friends of the Germans, whose language the young Swearingens learned, even the Low-German, and Swiss-German dialects. Then according to the report of our neighbor's son Sigismund Engelking, came Kleberg's brother-in-law, F. Engelking, who was married to a daughter of the von Roeder family, which had settled near Cat Spring in 1834; Karl Wennmohs, the Swiss brothers, Marcus and Fritz Amsler; Vornkahl; H. Bolten; the actor Louis Constant, who, according to reports, attempted to make Mill Creek navigable and who did other things that caused the neighbors to shake their heads in disapproval; Carpenter W. Mersmann; A. Hagemann, the inventor of tomato wine; F. Langhammer, who set up a tannery; the musically gifted Emil Kloss - it is said that he taught even his dogs to howl musically, and I can testify that they howled differently from any other dogs that I ever heard when they answered the wolves; his brother, the goldsmith, Robert Kloss; J.A. Wilm, who erected a gin driven by horses and mules; J.H. Krancher; Rudolph Goebel; the brothers Wilhelm and Carl Schneider from the Palatinate; August Goebel, who attained the age of ninety in good health and clarity of mind (his widow, Mrs. Helene Goebel, nee Roggemann, is still alive to tell of olden times in Millheim; Otto Goebel; F. Buntzel; Theodor Brosig, Dr. Carl Nagel; the teacher, E.G. Maetze; B. Siegert; A.F. Trenckmann; F: Heinecke; H. Kluever; if I am not mistaken, Millheim's first tailor - Riniker from Switzerland; and the skilled shoemaker Necker, who provided the neighborhood with shoes from leather tanned in Texas. For the most part they were young life-loving and enterprising people, and the bachelors among them were soon married. They learned to love their new home in spite of a meager income. There was little that could be sold for money. With the exception of a few like Emil Kloss, who became a wealthy man and spent the last half of his life on Lake Garda in Italy with his wife; Wennmohs; Dr. Nagel, and Constant, they remained in Millheim and found their last resting places in its sandy soil. Most of their descendants live in Millheim or in its vicinity today. I know of no other settlement in that part of the state from which so few have moved away. My old friend and first teacher, Mrs. Ida Schulze of Hempstead, told me during the recent Millheim festivities to honor the visiting Carl Nagel from St. Louis, who had served as Secretary of Commerce under Taft - the highest post attained by an Millheimer, that Adalbert Regenbrecht, then high in the seventies had said to her "In all the world there can't be a prettier place than Millheim." And Regenbrecht should know, as he hailed from the fine old city of Breslau. Certainly the old settlers had a discriminating eye for natural beauty and also for the practical values of a new place to locate. Millheim offered one advantage over the nearby Cat Spring. It was crossed by two clear steadily flowing creeks, each bordered at the lower end by forests. In the pamphlet "Austin County", which I published in 1899 and which furnished many accounts of Austin County and of the early days in Texas, Sigismund Engelking tells that in Clear Creek there was one deep swimming hole after another. Over this clear, never failing brook, wild peach trees made a leafy canopy to shut out every ray of the sun. When I was old enough to find the Paradise of my childhood in the creek, it was not so beautiful any more. The wild peach trees, which cannot bear to have the hoofs of cattle cutting into their fine roots, had almost disappeared, and the sand that had washed down from the cow trails on the hills and from the muchly traveled Houston road had filled up the water holes. Sometimes floods washed out these water holes, but they soon sanded up again. There I could build dams of sand for a shallow bathing pool that would fill up gradually and wash away with the first rain; but it was fun and building them over and over was a good lesson in perseverance. Similar conditions must have prevailed at Constant Creek farther to the west. But in nearby Mill Creek there was one water hole after another in which young Millheim could learn to swim and dive under the direction of the teacher and from which the anglers rarely returned without a rich haul of fish. The upper part of Millheim had hilly, black land, the center mixed soil, and the lower edge deep sand. Here began the great wide, gradually descending Gulf Prairie, on which until the 1870's one could have ridden to the Gulf on horseback without encountering a house or a fence. At that time it was assumed that this prairie, with its fine stand of grass would always provide free grazing for cattle, but this hope soon faded when the useful but hated freedom-restricting barbed wire made its appearance. Mill Creek Bottom provided much good wood, and was only a short distance away. Most valuable of all were the splendid white oaks, which furnished sturdy steps and shingles; the Spanish oaks, which were also suitable for shingles; the wild mulberries; which can be split so easily into durable fence posts, and the ash trees for wagon building. The post oak on the higher sandy soil furnished good fence rails and the wood from the hickory was used for yokes of oxen, ax handles, implement handles, and bows and cross bows for the boys. Half a dozen varieties of dewberries and blackberries furnished fruit from May until mid-summer. Mustang grapes were made into wine and wild plums in great abundance into delicious preserves. Ice cold springs burst forth on the hills in a number of places. Even the steep hill on the east side of Constant Creek, where the brakes always had to be used on the thrilling but scary downgrade, was valued by the settlers because in one of its steep slopes a hard cross-grained sandstone jutted out, which could be used for many purposes. Dr. Nagel built the first and the only remaining stone house in Millheim.

In his account of the baptism of the settlement, Sigismund Engelking, the jovial, phlegmatic humorist, who could see the funny side of just about anything, tells how merrily, even boisterously, things went on among the old - at that time almost all fairly young - Millheimers. He writes, "In the fifties a meeting was held in my father's first store, which he conducted in partnership with Nolte, for the purpose of giving our settlement a name, naturally I was a spectator, but I can't recall all the details. I do remember, however, that toward evening the meeting became very jolly. Barrels of tar were lighted and bets for wine and other drinks were made as to who could jump through the flames. A certain Quensel, also known as the Ranger, didn't jump high enough and fell into a burning barrel, searing his legs badly before the others could pull him out. Dr. Nagel smeared oil on his burns and the drinking and merriment, as well as the wrestling and racing went right on into the night. Dr. Nagel was the best jumper, and I always envied him for his achievements in this art. Such were the 'Schwabenstreichle', Swabian feats, in which the old Texans delighted."

During this hilarious meeting the name Muehlheim was chosen at the suggestion of Wilhelm Schneider, who came from the Rhine - Palatinate, but it wasn't long before the Anglo-Americans had botched it up into Millheim.

Naturally life in Millheim did not always run such a merry course, but on the whole, the settlers were a jolly folk, among whom a singing society soon came into being under the direction of schoolmaster Maetze, and many happy singing festivals were held. In origin the settlers were a motley company. The majority had originally been artisans; there was probably not one among them who had engaged in farming in Europe. They came from all German lands: the Amsler brothers, the dyer Hillboldt, the mason Hiltpold from the Canton Aargau, the tailor Riniker was also from Switzerland. Except in the school, where the teacher family insisted on High German, all sorts of dialects were common. Louis Kleberg, who died at an early age, Dr. Nagel, Regenbrecht, my father and surely Hagemann too had received a higher education; the brothers Kloss and J.H. Krancher had attended good city schools. Most of these educated men were somewhat better situated financially than their neighbors, but they were not in full command in Millheim. Genuine democracy prevailed. Just about everyone voiced and fought for his own opinion, and in the meetings where important matters were discussed my old friend Krancher, who though not highly schooled, was skilled in the use of tongue and pen, or the equally glib-tongued Carl Schneider, with his innate motherwit carried their opinion just as often as did the Lateiners; and it turned out that the artisans, to whom farming was an unknown calling too, got ahead faster than did the scholars, who tried to farm according to books published in Germany and England. Absolute sovereign in Millheim was only one man and, that man was our teacher E.G. Maetze, who reigned supreme in his own kingdom - the school.

To this school I shall have to devote separate space because it was the real heart and also the pride of the settlement. Old Millheim never had a church; and most of the Lateiners, my father being an exception, were even opposed to churches, as were the majority of the intellectuals of the Germany of that time. When as chairman of the school board, my father wanted to permit a wandering preacher to hold services in the schoolhouse, he was outvoted by his two colleagues, who insisted that a sermon would only create dissension in the otherwise so beautifully harmonious settlement. I was present at this meeting and heard the decision with my own ears. Millheim now has its fourth schoolhouse - with its school it has been moving slowly westward. The first schoolhouse had originally been the home of the Engelking family. It stood on their big farm and was well built.

A part of it had been used in the erection of a new home, the largest in the community, for the rapidly growing Engelking family. Ernst Gustav Maetze was the first teacher. He held his position for more than twenty-five years. A graduate in protestant theology of the University of Breslau, he is supposed to have preached only one sermon. Then he became principal of the public school, "Bürgerschule", in Bernstadt, Silesia. He played a leading part in the movement of eighteen-forty-eight. After Bismarck had became the forger of the German Reich, Maetze liked to recall the fact that in 1848 in the National Assembly in Berlin he had crossed verbal swords with the "Mad Junker". When reaction prevailed, Maetze had to flee. Coming to Texas, he earned his living for a while in New Ulm as a day laborer; but ill-fitted for plowing and rail splitting, he gladly accepted Mr. Engelking's invitation to come to Millheim and teach the latter's two elder sons and the sons of a few neighbors. His pupils increased fast in numbers. It did not take long for the news to spread that Millheim had an excellent teacher. Pupils came from great distances, for example, Rudolph Kleberg who was later elected to Congress; his brother Marcellus, who became a prominent attorney; and W.D. Cleveland, the son of a wealthy planter, who was for a long time one of the leading merchants in South Texas and who attributed much of his success to the knowledge of the German language that he had acquired in Millheim. Maetze impressed the Anglo-Americans too, who could not fail to respect the iron zeal which enabled his quick mastery of the English language. They called on him as a political speaker, and in time he was elected to the Senate of the State of Texas, where he was able to play an important role.

In a very few years the schoolhouse had become too small. Later it was used as a home for colored tenants. A new one was built between the Engelking and Kloss places. This burned down during the last half of the Civil War - the common theory being that it was set on fire as an act of vengeance by a passing soldier, an ex-pupil who like so many other young Texans had been unable to adjust himself to school discipline and had resented the rod. It was a different time in Texas. Most of the young men were either in the army or they were hauling cotton to Mexico for the government. Some were in hiding to evade the army service. Most of the fields lay uncultivated and what little was grown was unsalable. The Confederate paper money had become worthless, and the few who were somewhat better off had sacrificed their cash money to save ardent Unionists from being shot. At that time a new school building was not to be thought of. So school was held on the porch of the teacher's home, and on very cold days in his parlor. But as soon as peace reigned again and the few bales of cotton raised were for a short time bringing an excellent price - my father's gin book showed that in nine years the biggest yield of any one farm was three bales and most farms had produced only one - the word was "We must build a real schoolhouse." Money was still scarce but at a meeting which was held on the porch of my parents, I heard each man offer his contributions: one promised cash, another lumber hauled from Spring Creek, most offered their services in constructing the building.

On my first school day immediately after Easter in 1867, the schoolhouse, which afforded room for at least sixty children, had been in use for quite a while. Somewhat airy, since it had only been weatherboarded, it was certainly no palace; but we did not freeze because the nearby woods protected us from the north wind, and the iron stove gave off excellent heat. After a short time an inside wall and a small roof over the entrance were added and a rare thing in those days - it was provided with wall maps and a blackboard. An excellent practice introduced into this school as soon as circumstances permitted was that the tuition was paid on the first school day, if possible with a twenty-dollar gold piece. If I am not mistaken, another fine custom provided that the fourth child of a family of children attending school at the same time was given free tuition. Probably not one defaulted in paying the school money, since after twenty-seven years of teaching Maetze was able to retire in comfortable circumstances. In this respect Millheim was a model settlement. Today, forty years after his death, the memory of this teacher is honored by his pupils, even by those who felt his punishing hand.

# Excerpts from *A Boy's Civil War Story*

## by Charles Nagel

The following are selections from Charles Nagel's autobiographical book which has been republished on amazon.com by Stephen Engelking. Charles Nagel was the son of a doctor who practiced in Cat Spring and Millheim. The family were forced to leave Texas during the Civil War and ended up in Missouri where Charles became a famous politician, as his book relates.

## Millheim — The German Settlement

In a way there was nothing peculiar about this settlement in Austin County—named after the man who had helped pave the way for Houston's fame. But how different it seemed from the conditions we had left. There most of the neighbors seemed to be far away. True, Reichardt was nearby; farmer and stock raiser on a small scale. Also, Uncle Louis Litzman (mother's brother), a farmer in still more modest fashion, one too upon whose aid we could always count, as he could upon ours. Perhaps one or two more, comparative strangers. There was Himly whose name is like an echo, associated with books and like serious things. For aught we knew some may have been poets. Certainly imagination had had its part to prompt men and women to embark upon this Texas venture. And then fifteen miles away, Uncle Dittmar (husband of my mother's sister). He was a dear man, children loved him in spite of his fierce beard. People spoke of his beautiful tenor voice, which he no doubt had a better chance to exercise in those wilds than his profession of surveyor. He had cleared some ground in a remote forest of black jack oaks, where the squatter's title was perhaps more respected than any surveyor's certificate that he might give or receive. In most of these homes there were large families of children, but they had scarcely entered into our young lives.

It was very different in Millheim. Kloss, our neighbor in plain view, came from Rostock, near the Baltic. His neat home nestled among large trees. The abundance of flowers marked the foreigner, as his barn and his thriving field of grain and corn did the man of honest toil and fair training. He had had a city man's trade or profession; but the pioneer's ambition carried him over the top. Even the entrance to his barn was impressive. It had an arch over the gate. I should still feel that it must have been very high but for the memory of our neighbor's accident. His favorite horse ran away with one of the sons (our age). It came tearing past our house, and report said that finding the gate closed, the horse stopped so abruptly that the rider was not only unseated, but rose in the air over the arch and landed in the barnyard. All this was grist to our mill at the time. Relations with the neighbor's boys were rather strained at the moment. There had been a fight, two against two, about a rabbit in the hollow of a tree. The rabbit had escaped, and the fight had been a draw. Anything as humiliating to the enemy as being thrown by his own horse over the arch of the gate into a barnyard among cattle, hogs, and chickens, had a very soothing influence upon our lacerated nerves.

Most influential in our midst was Ernst Gustav Maetze, a graduate of Breslau, I believe; one of the many who had barely made the border after the revolution of 1848, and who was now to be our teacher, giving impressions and inspiration far beyond our youthful appreciation. His home, too, was almost hidden by trees. Shrubs and flowers greeted one at the front gate, and living chiefly by his profession, his garden was more important than his farm. It appears that Maetze had gone to New Ulm, and was working for a farmer when Engelking met him and induced him to come to Millheim as a tutor for his children—thus laying the foundation for what came to be our common school. If not a trained, he was a born teacher.

Next came Engelking, a graduate of Bonn, at law, I think, who now dispensed justice by giving fair measure in calicoes, ropes, molasses, coffee, etc., to the customers of his country store. Again the farm was an incident to his main business. He was married to a von Roeder, member of a family of nobility, some of whom had come early enough in the '30's to take part in the fight for Texas independence. Their house was exceptionally large, but not too large for the size of their family.

Another member of the Roeder family was married to Kleberg, a few miles beyond; the man of massive head, somewhat small stature and indomitable will. He, I think, was justice of the peace or notary public, but since law suits and legal forms were still spared our happy colony, we were wont to profit by his unofficial wisdom; and wonder at his daughter's beautiful name— Valeska.

Next to him, Trenckmann, proud proprietor of a grain mill, and the customary farm. A descendant is now the proprietor and editor of "Das Wochenblatt" published in Austin, Texas.

Farther away beyond "Dead Man's Creek," among others lived several branches of the Langhammer family, respected by all but at that time scarcely known to children.

Dead Man's Creek stood fully as ominous in our imagination as its name was unique. It was not a creek at all, but a trickling stream running through a marsh, with here and there a bog, which gave horse or mule a chance to prove his superior intelligence or instinct. Most points in a new country are associated with some story, either half true or the mere product of fancy. Dead Man's Creek had several, as so uncommon a name would suggest. That a man had been killed there no boy could doubt, but the incident was too remote to challenge our interest —perhaps Indians had done it. More authentic was the tale of the two men who had tried to quench their thirst at this stream. The first one lay down flat on the ground, but rested his arm on what he took to be the remnant of a tree. When the second one had got down, he suddenly jumped to his feet with the exclamation, "Gee, that is an alligator you have been resting on." "Is it?" was the answer, "I thought I heard something snore." We thought that a great story, and wondered at the inexperience of grown men. Finally there was the rumor that one family living on this creek insisted that there was no difference between chicken and snake meat, and we fancied that they were always eager to try it on people to convince them. We of course felt sure that this family was on the lookout for small boys as easiest victims, and Dead Man's Creek was one place at which we never tarried about meal time. Indeed, our minds were not quite at ease on the subject as it was. Before hearing of the story, we had taken a meal at one of these homes, and afterwards some one had said something about the whiteness and tenderness of snake meat. We suspected that we might have stood the ordeal once, but if so were the more resolved never to be caught again. Our imagination was so wrought upon that eels were regarded as little better than snakes; and for years frog legs had a narrow escape from the same judgment.

Immediately north was Hagemann, fair model for a picture of a prophet. He made a living for his family on his farm, raised very fine horses, and during the Civil War employed his training by making Rhine wine out of tomatoes,—a product which was unquestionably alluring to the eye, and was reluctantly admitted to be bearable to a starved taste.

In the other direction across the creek was Constant, who was said to be an actor by profession. He certainly seemed out of place off the stage. It is said that he planned to make Mill Creek navigable, when in some seasons we boys had to ride miles to find a hole with water enough to let us swim. Then there were the real farmers, the Hilboldts and Schneiders, one of whom restored to us the beautiful tenor lost in Dittmar, now far away in the forest. From what part of South Germany they came, I do not know; but there was no question of their loyalty to their particular dialect. Having been brought up to speak pure, almost Biblical German, dialect always left me in a bewildered state of mind, although even as a child I enjoyed the peculiar harmony of character and linguistic expression. Of this, Plattdeutsch (Low German) best understood by the North German, was a particular favorite, because mother could read it, so that I understood. To this day Fritz Reuter is a favorite with me. Few people know what they miss by not being able to enjoy his humor. I recall Schneider's appearance only faintly. But as long as memory lasts, I shall hear him sing with the enthusiasm of surrendering devotion those memorable words: "I b-i-i-n ein F-i-i-sch auf tro-o-ocknem S-a-and" (I am a fish on sand so dry); so suggestive of the actual state of some of our disillusioned newcomers, but really calculated to express a much more universal dilemma to which many Americans are now peculiarly sensitive.

To the south of us, just at the point where two branches of the forest reaching out from Mill Creek approach each other, leaving a gap to give us view of the endless prairie, lived Regenbrecht. He had married a Hagemann, and the family was large. He measured somewhere between six and seven feet, inclining to the latter I should say, and weighing not to exceed one hundred and sixty pounds if that much. He was college bred; was in the child's mind credited with rare intellectual powers and devoted his gifts to the not indifferent task of calculating the number of bushels to a small acreage; and whether the supply would last through the winter. Perhaps no one among us was better known for integrity and simplicity of character. He was a welcome visitor everywhere, always sure to brighten spare hours of my hard worked father in days when discussion and conversation were still counted among the social gifts. Less than a mile beyond lived Kluever; small but successful farmer.

All this sounds so simple and gives but a poor picture of the native beauty of the country, dotted with its unpretentious but well kept homes. It was all rather haphazard. The vegetable gardens were of course near the houses, because they had the personal attention if not care of the owners. Beyond that, however, there were pens for the domestic cattle, of which every home had some; and then fields of corn and even cotton, whose growth gave surest indication of the character of varying soils from richest black to poorest sand. But individuality marked location and development. No modern contractor's idea of symmetrical propriety had disturbed our conception of freedom of thought and conduct. This was before the farmer reversed the order of things to turn his place into a business for profit and from that profit to draw enough to feed and clothe his family. The family lived on and upon the farm — the surplus might yield a profit.

Finally, farthest south, on the very verge of the prairie extending far to the Gulf of Mexico as it were, the monarch of all he surveyed, lived Swearengen (Sam, I think). He was little known to us, but in many ways he was our accepted prototype. He stood alone, and I never look upon a picture of Washington now without going back to him — not the picture so much as what he stood for. He was not the only non-German but he was the one to whom we looked as a typical American. Perhaps we were influenced the more by his unwavering position as a Union man, when later on we of German blood were charged with the double complaint of being Union and German — in the parlance of the day, "Dutch" — a term to which we might not have objected, if its true dignity had been understood.

There were a few others of the older settlers not of German blood, but they were poor whites, rather contemptuously called "white trash." How they lived no one knew; they were not within our horizon. They were as clearly beneath our position as we (certainly after the secession issue was raised) were held in a separate caste by the more successful of the older stock. Perhaps one was as undeserved as the other. I do not recall that any of them were ever guilty of misconduct, and I have since then lived to learn that honesty and misfortune need not be strangers. However, Swearengen stood apart. He was a friend of Sam Houston—the idol of Texas youth; had fought with him as rumor went in the struggle for independence, and with him aided to oppose secession. He now lived the life of his conviction, a free American, with his wife, four sons and one daughter, about some of whom there will be more to tell. There were many others, but a youngster's memory is faulty, and some may come to me as I proceed.

Houston, sixty miles away to the east, then stood for but two ideas, the popular fame of Sam Houston, and the terror of yellow fever. If the fever did not prevail at all times, the danger of an outbreak seemed ever present. It touched us only as travelers passing our way made report, or threatened to carry the scourge. The long lines of covered wagons, as they crossed the plain, and as we see them pictured now, I never saw. But I saw enough to catch their spirit, and memory so gripped me that I was glad later in life to see their reproductions in the movie while the lights were down. For we saw the canvas wagons, usually in pairs, rising over the horizon and winding their weary way towards us along the dusty road, obdurate messengers of good or bad from the great world outside. As they came near us we could hear the rumbling of the wagons, the clanking of chains; could see the long and steady pull of the oxen under the burden of their heavy yokes, head down, long horned and varied in brands as in color; hear finally the strokes of the hoofs on the hard ground; the simple but persuasive "gee" or "haw" from the driver walking beside them, and perhaps the wicked crack of the cowhide whip hanging from the long elastic hickory handle. And then the wagons would stop, for here was the doctor's gate. At times there were only subdued conversations —not for us. At other times the drivers had symptoms that "allowed" examination. Then to our consternation these "suspects" would be taken into our sitting room to be examined, resting on the only lounge we owned. When the verdict was had—good or bad— there being no hospitals, the subject, with such remedies as could be given, went on his way, thinking no doubt that no symptoms was so much to the good, and trusting that bad symptoms did not always prove true; and father, a firm advocate of the theory that yellow fever could not be communicated by contact, would to our renewed terror, continue his much needed rest on the same and only lounge. The canvas wagons moved on, the oxen unmindful of the cause of their respite; and if the driver at last fell victim to the dread disease, perhaps there was no doctor's gate at which to stop, and probably enough in the then state of medical science, it made little difference. Those were the conditions as we saw them; wondering what could induce people to live in the presence of such danger all the time. That was part of the early story of Houston, splendid now in her prosperity, her attractive homes, her academy, her place as a great city of Texas—even of our country.

I can not believe that our settlement was closely associated with colonization schemes. It is true that father and mother, the Dittmars, Litzmanns and the Reichardts came from the same neighborhood abroad. But others came from very different parts of Germany, north and south; some like Amslin had even come from German Switzerland. I have the impression that Charles Sealsfield (author of books about Texas) was a name often mentioned in our home. Still later there came a considerable number of Bohemians. The two elements remained essentially apart, although the newcomers, too, had their castes. For instance, my uncle Litzmann's wife, "Tante Anna,"[63] was a Bohemian. Her charm and kindness won all children. My memory of her in later years, with her fair skin, arched brows, auburn hair and strangely gentle expression had me look upon the first canvas by Gabriel Max as an old acquaintance. Generally speaking, however, they provided for those who could afford such luxury, the farm labor and the maids, in which positions they were equally trustworthy and efficient. The German contingent of my

---

63 **Tanta** Anna: Austin County marriage records show that Frederick W. **Litzmann** married **Josepha** Anna **Wdral** on October 25, 1852. She is probably the **Ernst Bergmann** maid **Justina** that arrived in 1850 and was mentioned in his letter. The first large group of Czech settlers arrived in Cat Spring in April, 1852; no one with last name **Wdral** was among them.

memory, on the other hand, represented quite largely the professional class—men and women who had been driven to emigrate from conviction, moved by a demand for greater individual freedom and opportunity. They were not a reckless lot. They had at least attempted to reckon with the chances of their adventure. The impelling force of their hazardous undertaking was the same old dream of liberty which had prompted the earliest immigration to our country; and which we are still struggling to redeem. They were of a high order, moved by the spirit for sacrifice that sustained settlers in the earlier days. These impressions have of course come to me in later years. As a child I took it all for granted, and in any event had neither inducement nor standard for comparison.

But under the pressure of taunt and laughter that met me upon my rather pathetic appearance in the safe haven of the North after our escape from Texas, I began to suspect; and finally concluded that probably I had never been in a community of so high a percentage of college bred men as that from which the Civil War had driven us. My father, for illustration, was a graduate in medicine at Berlin, after having given some time to study for the clergy, including as I have been told even Hebrew. He was certainly at home in the Bible. They had suffered their disappointments; they had been forced to adopt unanticipated pursuits; but they had maintained their self-respect and offered a nucleus for the society of cultivated men and women. In the main a community of small farmers, with here and there as in my father's case a return to the original profession, they had found a happy, peace-loving society in which personal liberty and public order reigned supreme. These were the conditions into which our family had been transplanted (after their brief stay in Saint Bernardo) from old Germany.

## Our New Home in Millheim

The new home stood on the top of quite a hill— sandstone and generally poor soil—with its view down upon and into the forest in one direction, and prairie in the other. We were not so close up to wild life as we had been; but the challenge to imagination was greater, as was the chance for real encounter. It lay at the fork of two roads, one the main highway between Houston and Catspring, and farther west with a branch just beyond Constant Creek to Bellville; the other a road to San Felipe. This was a point of real advantage, for we could catch glimpses of the outside world, when modern townspeople can only watch the endless stretch of vehicles or automobiles. Apart from our unfailing interest in canvas covered wagons, there were cattle roaming free. It was for us to spot them and fix their ownership; and to wonder where a neighbor would catch up with a cow that was clearly going in the wrong direction. And then there were riders, some with common outfit bent on ordinary errands; others out for the joy of the ride. For instance, young Hagemann whose father raised the finest stock would pass the house on a spirited horse, with not a trick in saddle or bridle missing, as though his purpose in life was to arouse envy in the heart of an ambitious boy. Life was full of human incident, made richer by the view upon open spaces where eager eyes could often make out groups of deer peacefully grazing in the early morning or at dusk. Our entry into this home must have been very different from father's and mother's at Saint Bernardo. This time the house had been finished before we moved. Not so at the old place. After the terrible voyage from New Orleans to Galveston my parents had come to Houston, again by water through the now well developed bayou. From that point mother travelled by ox team, father having proceeded on horseback; and as though fate would give them no respite from their cruel hardships, they were overtaken by a severe Texas norther. Barring one night when mother and her party were taken in by a Good Samaritan, they were exposed to the cutting winds of the norther, the severity of which no one can know who has not felt it. After a day or two father returned to meet mother and they reached their destination chilled, and drenched from the exposure, with little or no preparation for their reception. Three families had jointly bought a common acreage. The agreement was that the land should be divided into three parts, and that the choice should be made by drawing lots, with the promise that he who drew the one habitable house should give shelter to the others as best he could until they could build their own homes. Reichart drew the home; and while father and mother did thus find protection with him during the day, they were forced to spend the nights in the one log house on their ground. This house had openings in the wall, but no windows; and its roof offered no serious hindrance to a fair view of moon and stars on clear nights, and as little to dew and rain on others. The redeeming feature of their experience was that the home was finally built as other difficulties were overcome; and that it was all done without so much as a rift in the relations between the parties to this quixotic enterprise.

But delighted as we were with our new home in Millheim, it is true that with all the university representation, we had as I recall it no architect. There must have been mechanics, and for the rest we probably relied upon the designs which were carried in memory, or suggested by what we saw before us. Perhaps some good angel had sent crude plans, not unlike the thoughtful Englishman who is said to have provided more or less perfect designs for New England colonies; for the comfort of early settlers and the admiration of intelligent visitors to this day. In no event were we in the competitive list with older settlers like Amslin, whose house had the air of a modern cottage nestling in the shade of protecting trees. But we managed to get our comfort, combined with utility, not unaided by American innovation. Our home was built very much upon the lines of the one at Saint Bernardo, with such additions as growing success would allow. There were the three main rooms, two bed rooms and one sitting room, which also served as dining room when season or inclement weather forbade the use of the porch with its glorious view through blossoming climbing roses, upon open space and the fields of corn and grain. For some time Paul and I slept in the third room, which was also the drug store. Often enough, half in sleep, have I seen mother with the old-fashioned scales in her hand and the trimly cut papers near by, measuring to fill the powders and salves according to father's prescriptions — the very picture of patient duty and loving devotion. Later on the drug store, true to custom, grew in size and variety. It encroached upon our space. Perhaps, too, the strong odors were disturbing. So the east porch was enclosed, and here we had three beds in a row along the blank wall, with quilts for warmth in winter, and with mattresses stuffed with corn shucks for comfort. It was marvelous how yielding the shucks became in a mattress when they had been so stubborn in the field. The size and shape of a boy was as it were faithfully reproduced by the impressions of his body. As time wore on, the undulations assumed shapes more and more fantastic, until a desperate director of a struggling museum might have been tempted to use such a mattress as a reduced model of an imposing mountain range. But at night we lost no sleep over them, and during the day they were discreetly covered with sheets or with cotton quilts — another of mother's many aids to our comfort. These had none of the allurements of crazy quilts. They were two plain sheets with cotton of our own picking, unadulterated by alien hand, between, stitched through to hold the cotton in place. Our house furniture was of the simplest, tables of plain wood, and chairs so straight and hard that later years may class them as rare, for no one would think of reproducing them. In the kitchen tin must have been the chief factor. This was certainly true of our wash bowls. Even so, they were sunk into the wash-stand to protect them from the hazards of awkward boys. We had soap, too, piled up in long pieces like cordwood, and handed out in chunks, cut off as necessity dictated. Soap was a domestic product. As I think of the large kettle with the heated conglomerate of grease and what not, forever seeking consistency under the stirring impetus of a paddle, I come to regard it as the first suggestion for the modern and little less seductive home brew. That soap was as uncompromising and unattractive as fundamentalism. It had no allurements for casual employment. It was meant to take off dirt and say nothing about it. It did both, and was a natural enemy of small boys. In making soap we were sometimes drafted into service. The paddle was entrusted to our hands, with the injunction to give that horrible brew no rest. This no doubt invited some resentment; but it was at all events work—dignified work that men might be asked to do. Very different was it when we were called upon to churn butter. No doubt the advent of woman's suffrage—the one human venture in which superiority persists by the side of equality—has changed all this. But in that age and generation it was the last word of humiliation to have a boy do work that by rights belonged to the feminine domain. To cook in camp was well enough; but to have to work in the kitchen was the limit. There are two things that can not be combined; and these are churning butter and getting lost in dreams. There is time for only one. If I were asked to name a job that would teach a scatterbrained lad the need for concentrated, continued and persistent effort for the accomplishment of a given task, I should say get a churn and put him to it. But we did not know our mercies; did not even know that we were spared the hair brush and to be honest, tooth brush, too. Perhaps that accounts for my full head of hair today, and for the dentist's statement that I have more teeth in my head than any of his patients of my age. But true to mother's rule, I must say "Unberufen" and rap on wood, as I do as I write. There must be some compensation in savage life. I take it ours was the fate of most country boys in the early days. The problem was during the warm season (which happily was long) to keep us out of water, and during the cooler season to get us into water. But that problem was not ours, except in so far as mother's watchful eyes curtailed our freedom of conduct. Perhaps she found some peace in the thought that whatever might be true of this season or that, the general average for the year was fairly good.

The third bed was Hermann Vahl's, an older boy whom father had taken in at the dying request of a stranger to whose aid he had been called at the last moment. It was an altruistic venture which no doubt gave Hermann more than he could have found elsewhere, but which certainly raised problems for our little family that might well have proved serious. Hermann was by nature alien to us; goodlooking as only the hero of romance can be; with the clear cut features of extreme southern type; brown eyes and dark hair with a certain wave. He was a born athlete, able to do most things by way of sport, and willing to do only a few by way of work. The very contrast of our common garden variety of cotton-haired boy of Nordic type.

The other bed room was father's and mother's, who had with them Baby Clara. Little Helene had died soon after our coming to Millheim, one Christmas Eve which, in memory of the peaceful little figure lying on our couch, has given Christmas a meaning of its own for me. My recollection of her is very vague, although I think of our playing with her in the open, and feeling a brother's joy in her merry laughter; or perhaps hearing a little cry at some mishap and being touched by her ready response to a brother's concern.

For the rest the house had a few changes from the old one. Above all, the larger fireplace, wide and deep enough for any hickory logs. There was no cellar, happily, for there were dark corners enough for timid boys with home-made candles that always blew out. The one lard lamp was not for us to meddle with. I only remember the scissor-like contraption to trim the wick; and the nut cracker—equal even to a hickory nut—both handmade of course, "made in Germany." The north porch served as our refrigerator. All water was hauled in a barrel laid on a sled, from the cold spring half way down the hill, and was left under the roof, away from the sun. The use of ice was not known to us. A cool spring was, therefore, of first importance, as was the sheltered porch on the north of the house. I remember seeing ice once, just enough to cover a sheet of water so close to the ground that the question of support did not arise. I tried to skate, sliding on the soles of my shoes; but the sliding was not restricted as I had figured and I was deterred from further serious efforts for life. A kitchen was added to the west, made of boards. Here the maid (for this was another new feature) reigned supreme; and here under her kindly care (she was

Bohemian) we snatched our hasty breakfasts of cornbread, fresh butter, New Orleans molasses, bacon and milk, before hurrying off for school. It was a great advance—too great to be just taken for granted even by boys given to trust Providence for all good things. But that was not all. We had a smoke house; another wooden addition. Just an enclosure as I see it with a door to enter, and cracks enough for well distributed ventilation. There was always meat enough on the hoof, but there was no Beef Baron to slaughter. To provide fresh beef or bacon was an event in the colony—fit suggestion for intelligent cooperation. Meats were obtained in larger quantity at one time, and were then kept by the several owners in the smoke houses to cure and to preserve. Hams and chunks of beef were hung from rods fastened across the smoke house and near the roof, to keep them within reach of the smoke and out of reach of such intruders as rats and mice. All this sounds very simple, but to cure meats is an art, and like most true arts, calls for care and patience. Anybody can start a fire, but very few know how to keep the hickory sticks alive—not enough to break into a blaze, and just enough to keep up a steady smoke to rise in even column up to the roof, there to envelop the suspended beef and bacon, and then to find its way out by the cracks in walls and roof. All the modem talk of smoke cured hams and nut fed hogs sounds like so much romance to me. It may all be true. But did we not have hogs that scarcely left two fighting boys enough pecans and hickory nuts to supply the family wants for the winter evenings before the blazing fireplace, undisturbed by family conflict as to who should place the log or stir the fire. And as for our smoke, no Cape Cod navigator could keep his pipe at a more steady draw. We have been taught to believe in, almost to worship progress; but there are some things in which wholesale production will never supplant or even touch the individual hand's creation. So at least I like to believe, in memory of the joys of my youth.

Another addition was the barn, surest proof of a farmer's rise to the test of success. When the barn looks smarter than the home, we know the owner's credit is good at the bank, although we may wonder a little about the care of his family, and be not so sure about the feeling of his neighbor. We had no such problems. Ours was just a fair barn built of logs, cracks plastered with mud and straw, enough to keep out most of the rain and draught; stalls enough for horses and mules, of which we had four or five, about which more hereafter. The loft right under the roof had space for corn and fodder, and here it was our joy in winter, when the fresh feed was wanting, to reach down to our pets—every horse and sometimes even a mule becomes a friend —their regular allowance of corn on the cob and dried corn stalk leaves tied in bundles, or hay for greedy meals. When I was there in 1909 that barn still stood, and the manger, out of which our horses were fed, was there intact though gnarled— silent testimony to the fibre of hickory wood. Attached to the barn was the common rail fence enclosure—pen we called it—in which the animals could move about when they were not let out into the larger pasture. Across the road, which passed just in front of the house—a thoroughfare all the way from Houston and then farther west—was another pen, larger, for into it we drove the cows for milking. There was room for many, because the Texas cow of that day was not equal as a milk producer to modern standards.

Just beyond was our garden rich in vegetables, and persuasive proof of the civilized taste and the achievements of foreign cultivation. There we had sweet peas, beans, radishes, turnips, cabbage, cucumbers, beets, sugar corn, Irish and sweet potatoes, onions, parsnips, cauliflower, carrots and squash. We even had asparagus; and well I remember father and mother working with spades to prepare the deep bed with well chosen soil. But asparagus after all remained a delicacy and was reserved for the grown ups, with no pangs to us, for vegetables as such were a disquieting incident in our lives. They seemed to be necessary for some people, and were forced upon us only as a customary urging of older people who professed to know what is good for boys. Somehow color almost as much as taste seems to decide a lad's like or dislike for food. There was—horrible to relate—even spinach standing menace of life, in youth and in old age. Hours of play I lost because I had the option to gaze upon the hated enemy all afternoon, rather than devour him at one desperate gulp. My dislike has never weakened; it was intensified; and to this day one of my nightmares takes shape in the doctor's order that I must at last, after a long battle of resistance come to spinach. So far I am thankful for my mercies. I can not believe that any one honestly likes spinach. When I see people eat it, disguised in milk or vinegar or other substitute, I firmly believe that their smug manner and patronizing look is nothing more or less than the eternal story of the fox's counsel with his tail cut off. For us a meal meant meat, beef or pork in all their forms, venison rarely, veal never, and bread and butter, molasses, brown sugar, with perhaps a potato (particularly a roasted sweet potato) thrown in. What more did man want here below?

Like all youngsters we had a sweet tooth for fruit. I think we had strawberries, but they, too, would go for a delicacy—fit morsel for older people. Our domain was the blackberry patch where sole competitors belonged to the animal world. We put up with wild persimmon ripened in the sun, if we got there before the opossum. Mustang grapes were symbolic rather with their strong vines reaching high up into the oaks, and serving as ornaments to the tree and as swings for adventurous boys. We ate sweet peas in the shell, before they were spoiled by cooking. Sugar corn was a favorite. We would cut the stalk just as the tassel indicated that it was ripening, then strip off the outer rind and chew the rest for the sugar that it contained. The process did not quite lend itself to modern form. But boldfaced chewing was not frowned upon then as it is now, although I am sure we got more out of it than later custom yields. Tobacco chewing was never adopted by the original immigrants. As a native I was made immune by an early and most unhappy experiment —of course under the influence of a dare. And after all, be it tobacco or gum it is chewing still—a habit condemned but not abandoned. We had plums, cherries, I think, and peaches. Children have them in the cities now, picked by other hands, and trusted to ripen in the market. It was our joy to know when they would ripen, and to get them before some one else crossed our purpose. Peaches were the prize fruit, and of these we had great red faced cling stones — Indian peach, we called them. The earliest could be picked from the hanging branches; others by climbing into the tree to reach for those near enough to the trunk or strong branch. But there was only one ideal way; for it marked the boys' advantage. Peaches are still my passion; but I eat them now seeing myself standing in the saddle, my horse under the tree, reaching out for the red cheeked fruit, immune from common touch; to collect them into my hickory shirt, and to enjoy them on my ride. Probably a magnet of every boy's eye was the watermelon. We had very few of the long cucumber shaped melon. Ours belonged to the cannon ball type, of one color, darkest green. We would watch the ripening process with the care of a modem devotee of research — deepening color, state of the vine; until it came to the final test. Some would make it by cutting a small triangular hole into the melon, and drawing out a sample for inspection. But no real worshiper of the melon would use methods so crude, and so sure to injure the fruit if opened too soon, even in so slight a manner. Our method was simple and I think true. Of course, we did as our elders did. We struck the melon with our little knuckles, and looked wise with a far away look as we listened to the sound. But that was not the real test. We touched the vine just where it was attached to the melon. If it snapped the fruit was ripe. If not, the proof was clear — the melon was still drawing sustenance from the vine. But to be sure of the test it was made early in the morning while the dew was still upon the plants; for later in the day under the hot and drying sun even a green vine might snap. We lived by this rule until watermelon later in the season or by the aid of marauders became more scarce. I will not say that under such pressure we did not sometimes welcome the aid of the drying sun, and did not perhaps give the vine a special tug. But even so, true to the methods of modern statesmanship we might neglect the spirit, but we always respected the letter, and we never lost the substance. With that intuition which makes the only true rules of conduct, we aimed to gather our melon in the early morning while the test was sure, and while the fruit itself was cool from the night's exposure. Then it was placed in our cool spring, to be taken out at the proper time. Sometimes we carried melons on our expeditions for several miles, holding them in our hands over the saddle knobs, and cooling them in a stream, for dessert after the swim and camp meal. City people may think they know what watermelon is. They eat them in our clubs as though they did. Often have I tried it in the attempt to fool myself back into the illusions of youth. But too often the melons are spongy, and do not dissolve like sugar on the tongue. He who as a boy has put his knife into the rind of a melon and has seen the running crack in response to the cut; who has had the luscious heart of a melon melt on his palate, will no more be deceived by a battered victim of modern traffic, than will he who has tasted a Rockyford in Colorado or Utah, be intrigued by the cross of melon and squash that is so often served to us. Even today a farmer's life has its advantages, its charm and its pleasures past compare.

# Articles and Book Excerpts About Cat Spring and Millheim

Robert Kleberg Justus, Sr. wrote his memoirs which were published in 1880 as a chapter in the book *Indian Wars and Pioneers of Texas*, by John Henry Brown. (This can be found on page 189).

Rosalie ("Rosa") von Roeder Kleberg, wife of Robert Justus Kleberg, Sr., wrote "Some of My Earliest Experiences in Texas". It was published in the April, 1898 issue of the *Southwestern Historical Quarterly*. It is appended.

Ottilie Fuchs Goeth wrote *Memoirs of a Texas Grandmother,* in 1915 in which she described her childhood experiences in Cat Spring. Pertinent excerpts from this book are appended.

Caroline Ernst von Hinueber wrote of her experiences in the early days of Industry in "Life of German Pioneers in Early Texas", published in the January, 1899 edition of the *Southwestern Historical Quarterly*. It is appended.

Adalbert Regenbrecht wrote "The German Settlers of Millheim (Texas) Before the Civil War". It published in the July, 1916 *Southwestern Historical Quarterly*. It is appended.

*The Cat Spring Story* and *Century of Agricultural Progress: Minutes of the Cat Spring Agricultural Society: 1856 - 1956* were published by the Society in 1956.

Ann and James Lindemann and William Richter in 1986 published *Historical Accounts of Industry, Texas: 1831 - 1986.*

Flora von Roeder published *These Are the Generations* in two volumes in 2014. These books present outstandingly researched genealogy of the extended von Roeder family, which include many of the original Cat Spring and Millheim residents such as Klebergs and Engelkings. Her books are available on amazon.com.

A brief biography of Senator Gustav Maetze was in included in Personnel of the Texas State Government with Sketches of Distinguished Texans, compiled by L.E. Daniell (Austin, Smith, Hicks and Jones, 1889). It can be found on page 88.

# Literary Works by Cat Spring and Millheim Residents

Charles Nagel wrote *A Boy's Civil War Story* in 1935. The first half of this book tells of his childhood days in Millheim before and during the Civil War. It has been annotated and republished on amazon.com by Steve Engelking in 2017. A segment of this can be found on page 219.

William Andreas Trenckmann was a prolific writer born and raised in Millheim. He published a German language newspaper in Bellville and Austin between 1891 and 1933. During this period he wrote and published supplements to his newspaper. Some were historical in nature and allegorical books and plays he had written. Trenckmann's literary works are summarized as:

*The History of Austin County, Texas.* 1891. Annotated and republished on amazon.com by Steven Engelking in 2015.

*Christmas in Troubled Times.* 1893. Appended.

*The Schoolmasters of New Rostock, a Texas Folk Play in Two Acts.* 1903. Appended.

*Pioneer Times at the A. and M.* 1907. Appended.

*Experiences and Observations.* 1931 - 1933. Annotated and republished on amazon.com by James Woodrick in 2015. This can be found on page 209.

*Die Latiener am Possum Creek* (originally published 1908 as a series in *Das Bellville Wochenblatt*). Translation and manuscript in progress by James Kearney with a planned publication date of 2018.

Johannes Christleib Nathanael Romberg, called the German Poet Laureate of Texas, lived in the Cat Spring area for six years after immigration. A collection of his poems was published under the title *Gedichte von (Poems of) Johannes Romberg* in 1900 by E. Pierson of Dresden and Leipzig. It was translated and republished by his great-grandson Friedrich Ernst Romberg in 1990.

Adoph Fuchs lived in Cat Spring for eight years. He was a poet, novelist and songwriter. He published a poem in 1836 titled *The New Fatherland,* and a book titled *Robert* in 1842. Both were critical of the German politics at that time and spoke of emigration to America. He also left a 119 page bound book containing the words and lyrics to songs he composed.[64]

---

64 The original songbook and many other family memorabilia is located in the Adolph Fuchs Family Papers, archive box 2E367, Briscoe Center for American History, The University of Texas at Austin.

# Bibliography / Related Reading

Austin County Historical Commission, *Education in Austin County Vol. I The Era Prior to 1885* (Published by the Commission in 1997).

Biesele, R.L., *The History of the German Settlements in Texas*, von Beckman Jones, Austin, 1930. Online at: https://babel.hathitrust.org/cgi/pt?id=inu.32000006737268;view=1up;seq=13

Brown, John Henry, "Robert Justus Kleberg", a chapter in *Indian Wars and Pioneers of Texas* (Austin, L.E. Daniells, 1880).

Cat Spring Agricultural Society:

*The Cat Spring Story* (San Antonio, Lone Star Printing Company, 1956)

*Century of Agricultural Progress: 1856 - 1956, Minutes of the Cat Spring Agricultural Society* (San Antonio, Lone Star Printing Company, 1956)

Engelking, Friedrich Ferdinand, *The Engelking Letters*, translated by Flora von Roeder and edited by Steven Engelking (Tuningen, Germany, The Hugh & Helene Schonfeld World Service Trust, 2012)

*Frizzell*, Isabel, Bellville: *The Founders and Their Legacy* (New Ulm, Texas, New Ulm Enterprise Print, 1992)

Goeth, Otilie Fuchs, *Memoirs of a Texas Pioneer Grandmother.* Originally written in 1915, translated by Irma Goeth Guenther in 1969, first published by Eakin Press (Austin) in 1982, revised and reformatted by Kenneth W. Fuchs in 2010.

Handbook of Texas Online, by the Texas State Historical Association. Contains numerous articles about Cat Spring and Millheim, and many of the early pioneers and noted individuals of that area.

von Hinueber, Caroline Ernst, "Life of German Pioneers in Early Texas", *Southwestern Historical Quarterly*, Volume 2, January 1899, pp. 227 - 232.

Kleberg, Rosa, "Some of My Earliest Experiences in Texas", Southwestern Historical Quarterly, Volume 1, April 1898, pp. 297 – 302.

Lindemann, Ann and James, and William Richter, *Historical Accounts of Industry, Texas: 1831 - 1986* (New Ulm, Texas, New Ulm Enterprise Print, 1986)

Murray, Joyce, *Austin County, Texas Deed Abstracts: 1837 - 1852* (Wolfe City, Texas, Henington Publishing Co, 1987)

Nagel, Charles, *A Boy's Civil War Story* (St. Louis, Eden Publishing Co., 1935).

Ragsdale, Crystal Sass, *The Golden Free Land: The Reminiscences and Letters of Women on an American Frontier* (Austin, Landmark Press, 1976)

Regenbrecht, Adalbert, "The German Settlers of Millheim (Texas) Before the Civil War", *Southwestern Historical Quarterly*, Volume 20, No. 1, July 1916, pp. 28 – 34.

von Roeder, Flora, *These Are The Generations: A Biography of the Von Roeder Family and its Role in Texas History*, in two volumes (self-published on amazon.com in 2014)

Romberg, Johannes Christliebe Nathanael, *Gedichte von Johannes Romberg*. (Dresden and Leipzig, E. Pierson Co., 1900).

Schuette, Arthur L., *The German Settlers of Cat Spring and Their Scientific Study of Agriculture*. Master's Degree thesis at Southwest Texas State Teachers College, August, 1945. Available online at: http://columbustexas.net/library/manuscripts/Ms%2024.htm.

Stoehr, Louise Ernst, "Die Erste Deutsch Frau in Texas", *Deutsch Pioneer* 16 (1884): 372 - 375.

Tiling, Moritz, *German Elements in Texas*, Moritz Publishing Company, Houston, 1913. Republished on Amazon.com by Stephen Engelking.

Trenckmann, William Andreas:

*The History of Austin County, Texas*. Initially published in German as a supplement to the Bellville Wochenblatt in 1891. Translated by William, Else and Clara Trenckmann, edited and republished on amazon.com by Steven Engelking in 2015.

*Christmas in Troubled Times*. Initially published in German in the Bellville Wochenblatt on December 3, 1893, translated by Anders Saustrup, published by The Friends of Weindale, Round Top, in 1976, and in The Journal of the German-Texan Heritage Society, Volume XXX, Number 4, Winter 2008.

*The Schoolmasters of New Rostock, a Texas Folk Play in Two Acts*. Printed in a supplement to the Bellville Wochenblatt, December 24, 1903, translated by Hubert P. Heinen and published in the Newsletter of the German-Texan Heritage Society, Volume VIII, Number 3, Fall 1986.

*Pioneer Times at the A. and M.* Published in Long Horn, the yearbook of Texas A&M College, 1907.

*Experiences and Observations*. Initially published in the Austin, Texas German-language newspaper *Das Wochenblatt* as a series between 1931 and 1933. Translated by William, Else and Clara Trenckmann, edited and republished on amazon.com by James Woodrick in 2015.

*Die Latiener am Possum Creek.* Translation and editing in progress by James Kearney, publication planned for 2018.

www.ingramcontent.com/pod-product-compliance
Lightning Source LLC
Chambersburg PA
CBHW052100280426
43673CB00070B/29